WELL & FAITHFULLY DISCHARGED

WELL & FAITHFULLY DISCHARGED

FINANCIAL TTP FOR MILITARY RETIREMENT

Curt Sheldon, CFP®

ISBN-13: 9781548890087
ISBN-10: 1548890081
Library of Congress Control Number: 2017911191
CreateSpace Independent Publishing Platform
North Charleston, South Carolina

For my wife Cathy who served this great nation with me for 24 years and has put up with me for over 30. She is truly the best thing that ever happened to me.

TABLE OF CONTENTS

CHAPTER 1

WELCOME TO THE FUTURE

I t was just yesterday that you pinned on those "butter bars" or sewed on your first stripes, wasn't it? I know it was for me. Now you're seriously looking at the reality that in the not too distant future you're going to be hanging up your uniform one last time. Leaving the military after spending virtually your entire adult life in it can be a challenging experience. Not only can it be challenging, it will change your financial life.

That change is what this book is about–helping you work through the financial changes you are about to experience. It will give you some techniques, tactics and procedures you can use in your transition and also some thoughts to help you make tough decisions.

When I was a young pilot, I was taught a cross-check that would help me fly at low-altitude and accomplish the mission safely. I'm pretty sure all the services have a similar mindset. I remember my Army brethren talking about handling the 15-meter target first. In any event, for me, the cross-check went like this: *Near rocks...Far rocks...Lead...Check-6,* and it meant the following:

- **Near Rocks.** What things are in my flight path right now? What do I need to correct to keep me from getting hurt?
- **Far Rocks.** What is out there on the horizon that I should start planning for?

- **Lead**. Am I where I'm supposed to be? Do I need to make a correction? How is the boss doing?
- **Check-6**. What unexpected thing out there might sneak up on me and really hurt me?

I'll use this framework to talk about your financial transition.

- **Near Rocks.** What financial decisions do I have to make and what actions do I have to take before or right after I retire?
- **Far Rocks.** What actions should I be taking to get my financial house in order? What things are out there in the distant future I should start thinking about?
- **Lead.** My potential new boss is offering me a lot of different employee benefits. What do they all mean to me? What if I go into business for myself?
- **Check-6.** What financial traps are out there waiting for me? What do I need to watch out for?

So, what do you say we start the mission of your financial transition?

CHAPTER 2

NEAR ROCKS

What is out there that you need to take care of now before you retire or pretty soon after you hang up your uniform the last time? To start with, you'll need to set things up to take care of your family if something were to happen to you. You'll also need to make decisions about your health care, and of course, you'll have to decide about some no-kidding dollar and cents issues as well.

Survivor Benefit Plan

Before you can retire, you will be required to make a decision about your Survivor Benefit Plan (SBP). Actually, that isn't 100% correct. If you are married, your spouse will have to make a decision about SBP. If you elect anything other than full coverage for your spouse, your spouse will have to agree, in writing, to the reduction. So, to a certain extent, the decision is your spouse's to make. But before I talk about this decision, I'll review what SBP is.

I often hear, "SBP is just life insurance and that's it." Not really. SBP is more akin to a joint and survivor annuity, and in reality all Qualified Defined Benefit Pension Plans[1] have the same

---

1 I'll explain qualified retirement plans in Chapter 4, Lead.

requirements...a minimum spousal benefit that only the spouse can decline. So let's frame SBP in that manner. If you select SBP, you agree to a smaller pension payment now in exchange for a pension payment for your spouse in the future (assuming you die first).

Full SBP benefits are 55% of your full pension payment. You can't get more than that, even if you would like. But you can elect an amount less than your full benefit. The amount you select, ranging from your full retirement pay to a minimum of $300 a month is called your *base amount*. The amount your surviving spouse will receive is 55% of the base amount, again ranging from 55% of your full retirement pay to 55% of $300 per month. Once you designate the base amount, it is set...in stone. With that said, the base amount will increase to the same extent your retirement pay does (and other government benefits such as Social Security). Another way to say that is that SBP benefits are inflation adjusted. Of course to get this benefit, you must accept a reduced pension.

How much will your retirement be reduced? It depends on the benefit you select. The formula used to calculate the reduction is:

Pension Reduction = (Base Amount) x 6.5%

So, how much might that be for you? (These numbers, which are summarized in Table 1, are approximate, your exact reduction will depend on your actual retirement pay.) An O-6 retiring with 30 years of service and selecting full benefits (55%) of retired pay would see his or her retirement pay get reduced from $8,053 per month to $7,355. Upon the retired member's passing, the surviving spouse would receive $4,429 per month. In the case of an E-9 retiring with 30 years of service and selecting full benefit, that member's retirement pay would be reduced from $4,913 to $4,487 per month, and a surviving spouse would receive $2,702 per month.

Table 1: SBP Calculations for Retiring Service Members Selecting Full Benefits

Rank and Years in Service	Retirement Pay*	Reduced Retirement Pay*	Spousal Benefits*
O-6 with 30	$8,053	$7,355	$4,429
E-9 with 30	$4,913	$4,487	$2,702

*Values are per month.

On the low end, the minimum benefit ($300 base amount) would lower retirement pay by $7.50[2] per month and the benefit for a surviving spouse would be $165 per month. Remember, these reductions continue for 30 years or until you reach age 70, which-ever is later. The reduction in your retiree pay will show up on your Retiree Account Statement (RAS) as a deduction, but remember, we're not going to think about it that way.

Should You Select SBP?

To answer the question as to whether you should take SBP or replace it with an insurance product or investments, you must first accurately answer four relatively simple questions. I've left space for you to fill in the answers.

When are you going to die? _____

When is your spouse going to die? _____

What will be the inflation rate until the above occur?

_____

What will you earn on your investments during both lifes-pans? _____

---

2 For base amounts less than $635 per month (inflation adjusted) the formula for calculating the retirement pay reduction is different. It approximates 2.5% of elected base amounts for low amounts. See http://militarypay.defense.gov/survivor/sbp/04_cost_spouse.html for further details.

I know, I know. You can't accurately answer these questions. But, these questions illustrate the risks you accept when you try to replace SBP with insurance: inflation risk and longevity risk. *Inflation risk* is the risk that your investments will not accrue earnings or interest at an amount that exceeds inflation by the amount planned. When talking about insurance, inflation risk is the risk that inflation will be higher than planned for, and your insurance death benefit will have less buying power than you had estimated.

Longevity risk is the risk that your surviving spouse (in this case) will outlive the money invested or paid by insurance. But rather than talk in abstract terms, let's take a look at a couple of different scenarios.

Once you answer the above questions, you can draw up your plan, and let's face it, military members can draw up a plan. Suppose you come up with the following answers to the questions for your worst-case scenario.

- I will die 20 years after I retire.
- My spouse will die 20 years after me.
- Inflation will be 3% throughout the duration of the plan.
- Investments will earn 5.073% throughout the duration of the plan.

Life happens...

- As a good military member (retired), you execute the plan and die exactly 20 years after your retirement.
- As a good military spouse, your spouse executes the plan and dies exactly 20 years after you do.
- You earn exactly 5.073% on your investments.
- The only thing you get wrong is that during your life (20 years) the inflation rate is 4% rather than the 3% you predicted. The second you die, the inflation rate pops back to 3%.

Result: Your spouse will live out the rest of his or her life on 16% less income than you planned. In other words, if you planned to provide your spouse $80,000 per year in future spending, due to the increased inflation, that $80,000 will only buy $67,200 in goods and services.

The above scenario assumes you nearly perfectly predict the future. What if you miss it big-time?

- You die 1 day after your 20-year term insurance[3] policy expires. (You bought term and invested the difference right?)
- Your spouse decides to ignore the plan and lives to his or her 10th percentile life expectancy of 98 for a male or 100 for a female.
- The day after you die, the market starts a major correction. Consequently, your portfolio goes down in value by about 30%, making it unable to pay out as planned. The money is not sufficient to last for your spouse's remaining 30+ years of life and maintain his or her standard of living.
- Ah heck, I'll throw you a bone…you get the inflation rate correct.

The reality can be pretty eye-opening. While both men and women are affected by longevity and inflation risk, women are more likely to be affected by these risks due to the facts that they generally have longer life expectancies. Today, in modern America, the median income for women age 85 and over is $15,248. Basically Social Security. Are you willing to ask your spouse to accept that risk?

---

3 Term insurance is life insurance that will pay if you die during the term of the policy (20 years as an example). If you pass away after the term ends, there is no payment.

Yea, But My Buddy Said...

There are a lot of barracks lawyers out there, and you'll get plenty of advice on LinkedIn or other social sites about what you should do. You'll have to decide whether you want to take that advice or not. But here are a couple of comments I've heard and some thoughts about them.

"Life insurance proceeds are tax free, SBP payments are taxable, so you want life insurance." This statement is true, as far as it goes. Life insurance proceeds are _income tax_ free (they could be subject to estate tax). But what is the beneficiary going to do with the life insurance proceeds? Most likely invest them. And those investments will generate income that will be taxable. In fact, if the portfolio is going to be sustainable over a long period, then the majority of the withdrawal from the portfolio for living expenses will be earnings...and taxable.

"If my spouse dies first, I've wasted my money." Let me answer this one with a question. Did you have a car accident yesterday? If not, then you "wasted" your money on your auto insurance premiums (for that day). The SBP decision is not a decision about making money, but rather it is a decision concerning risk transfer. In other words, are you are willing to pay the government to accept longevity and inflation risk for your spouse?

"I can buy life insurance for less money." Or the variation, *"I can buy a million dollar policy for less than what SBP costs."* The first thought I would have on this statement is, "Are you sure you're comparing apples to apples?" For a "fair" cost comparison you need to compare SBP with a whole life policy (with all premiums paid by the 30 year point). Then I would ask the question, "How are you going to mitigate longevity, inflation, and return sequence (the market crash scenario) risks?" Or in other words, "How do you know $1 million (or whatever the number is) is enough?"

So, It's a "No-Brainer," Right?

I don't think there is such a thing as a "no-brainer." But, my best "military advice" is to think long and hard before you decline SBP unless you have a compelling reason not to take it or a portfolio well into seven figures.

With that said, there are times when SBP might not be the right decision for you:

- Your spouse already has a lifetime source of inflation-adjusted income. This might be the case when a military member is married to another military member who will also retire. Military married to a civil servant, teacher, or someone with a good pension might also fit the bill. If your spouse has a significant pension available, SBP might not be indicated. Be sure to check to see if the pension increases with inflation. (Most non-governmental pensions do not increase with inflation.). If your spouse has a lifetime source of income, see the decision tree in Appendix A to help you determine if SBP is appropriate.

- You may have heard (and I used to teach) that naming a special needs child as an SBP beneficiary is not a good idea as the child's resulting income would disqualify him or her from state aid based on need. In fact, that is still true. But, recent legislation allows you to name a special needs trust as a SBP beneficiary. This could make sense. But before you go down this path, make sure that you consult with a qualified special needs planning attorney or financial planner.

Also, don't make the assumption that SBP will be sufficient. Depending on your lifestyle, additional protection (probably through insurance) might be necessary. How do you know? Take the time to figure out what the essential living expenses will be when you pass. There isn't a set formula for this, it depends on your own values. Then take a look at whether SBP plus Social Security will cover these expenses. Remember, the earliest your spouse can claim Social Security widow's benefits is age 60, so account for that too. If those guaranteed sources of income won't be enough, you might want to consider another tool to add to the toolbox to cover these expenses. In many cases this could involve a combination of life insurance and an immediate annuity.

If you're really getting hung up on the expense and considering life insurance instead, see Appendix B.

One More Thing

As an "annuitant" (someone receiving a government pension), you are eligible for the Federal Government's Long-Term Care Insurance Program. This is also true for your surviving spouse if he or she is receiving SBP benefits. If not receiving SBP benefits, your surviving spouse is not eligible for the program. If your spouse is forced to buy a policy on the commercial market, this could result in a significant increase in premiums. Because the Federal insurance program prices in a gender-neutral fashion, this could be especially expensive for a female spouse. For most commercially available policies, price is based on gender, and women, especially widowed women, pay significantly higher premiums.

Dependent Indemnity Compensation

It is possible your spouse could qualify for Dependent Indemnity Compensation (DIC). DIC is paid to the survivors of deceased veterans who die of a service-connected cause. Once a member has retired, that person's death will be considered to be service-connected if the cause of death is due to an injury or disease contracted while the member was on active duty.

Additionally, DIC may be paid if:

- The member had a 100% VA disability rating for 10 or more continuous years immediately preceding death.
- The member had a 100% VA disability rating for at least 5 continuous years, and the 100% disability rating was awarded immediately upon retirement.
- The member had a 100% VA disability rating for at least 1 year immediately preceding death, the member was a former prisoner of war, and death occurred after September 30, 1999.

DIC is only paid if your surviving spouse applies to the VA. SBP payments are reduced by the amount of DIC received[4]. The good news is since DIC is a VA benefit, it is tax-free. There is also the Special Survivor Indemnity Allowance (SSIA). SSIA is paid to surviving spouses who receive SBP payments and also receive DIC[5]. SSIA was scheduled to expire on October 1, 2017, but the 2017 National Defense Authorization Act (NDAA) extended SSIA until May 2018[6].

Savings Bonds

If you purchased savings bonds to pay for a child's college education, *you probably should take action before you retire.* One of the advantages of using savings bonds to pay for college is the interest can be tax free as long as the bond proceeds are used for qualified education expenses[7]. The problem with tax breaks is this: "As the

---

4 As of this writing, the basic monthly rate for DIC is $1,215. There are additions for totally disabled veterans, deceased veterans with dependents under age 18, and others. For further details see http://www.benefits.va.gov/COMPENSATION/resources_comp03.asp#BM01

5 SSIA is currently $275 per month.

6 http://www.moaa.org/Content/Publications-and-Media/Press-Releases/Detail/MOAA-Responds-to-2017-Defense-Bill.aspx

7 There are several requirements on savings bonds; three key requirements are: (1) The bonds must have been issued after 1989 in the name of the tax-

IRS giveth, the IRS taketh away." The ability to withdraw the funds tax free is eliminated if your Modified Adjusted Gross Income exceeds $147,250 if your filing status is married filing jointly. or $93,150 if filing single[8]. (Your Adjusted Gross Income or AGI, the number on the last line of the first page of your form 1040, is a good number to figure out if you are close to the limit.) The tax break starts to phase out at $117,250 if your status is married filing jointly, or $78,150 if filing single. So if you're still on active duty, and especially if you are an E-9, you might want to cash out the savings bonds before you get your new job on the outside and your income exceeds the limits.

But some of you are saying to yourself, "My kids are 5 years away from college, won't I have to pay taxes on the distribution?" I have some good news. You are allowed to cash the savings bonds and deposit the proceeds into a 529 account without having to pay taxes on the income. This is because contributions to a 529 plan are considered a qualified education expense, however the plan must be for yourself, your spouse, or a dependent[9]. Remember, there is a pretty good chance you won't be able to do this after you get your job on the outside.

Replacing SGLI

Most likely you have Servicemembers Group Life Insurance (SGLI). SGLI is a good insurance program, but since you will no longer be a Servicemember after you retire, your insurance coverage will end when you retire. Actually, SGLI will stay in force for 120 days after you retire. This is to allow you time to find a replacement

---

payer; (2) the taxpayer must have been age 24 or older when the bonds were issued; and (3) the taxpayer must be using a filing status other than Married Filing Separately.

8 2017 amounts

9 See IRS Pub 970: https://www.irs.gov/pub/irs-pdf/p970.pdf.

for your coverage. When looking for a replacement, keep this in mind: A basic tenet of insurance is to transfer the risk of events you cannot afford to accept–such as pre-mature death—to another entity. As an example, we insure our cars for the unlikely event we will have an accident and need to repair the car or pay for medical expenses/property damage, _not_ for such things as oil changes or new tires. In the case of life insurance, the question becomes: What reduction in lifestyle is your spouse willing to accept?

One option you will have is the Veteran's Group Life Insurance (VGLI) program. Just because you can select VGLI, it doesn't mean you should. VGLI has one significant advantage over other insurance programs/policies. If you apply within the specified time, 240 days from your date of separation, you will not have to answer any health questions. Therefore, you will receive coverage regardless of your health. Of course, this benefit comes with a cost; Table 2 shows the current monthly premiums[10]. For a relatively healthy individual at retirement age, commercial policies are available at a lower cost. Remember, like a 5-year renewable term policy, premiums increase as you age, even if you already have coverage in place.

Table 2: Current (2017) VGLI Monthly Premiums

Age	Amount
40-44	$68.00
45-49	$88.00
50-54	$144.00
55-59	$268.00
60-64	$432.00
65-69	$600.00
70-74	$920.00
75 & above	$1,840.00

10 Current as of January 2017. Assumes $400,000 coverage. Premiums are monthly. For more information, go to http://www.benefits.va.gov/INSUR-ANCE/vgli_rates_new.asp

If VGLI is not the right answer for you, what type of insurance and how much should you buy? Let's begin with the amount. If SBP and Social Security, when available, will provide for an acceptable standard of living, then you might not need any life insurance, or the need might be for a relatively short time. If there is an income/expense "gap," then you need to fill that gap with insurance. And, by the way, when calculating the insurance need, we assume you will get hit by a bus today.

The type of insurance depends on the answer to this question: Is the insurance for _when_ you die or _if_ you die? Now, I know some of you are saying, "What? We're all going to die." I know. But, the financial risk from the death might be time limited. So, if the insurance need is for _if_ you die before a certain event/date, then a term solution might be the better option. If the insurance is for _when_ you die, regardless of when death occurs, then a permanent product (whole life, universal life, etc.) might be a better choice. For example:

- If I die before Junior finishes college, my family will need funds to pay for school, then term makes sense.
- If I die before my spouse reaches age 60 (and becomes eligible for Social Security widow's benefits), my spouse will need funds to supplement SBP; again, term makes good sense.
- When I die, my estate will need funds to buy out my business partner (or pay estate taxes); then a permanent product might be the better choice.

Decide About TRICARE

You're going to have to do something you've never done before…at least not while you were on active duty—decide about medical insurance. Your spouse and family are probably already used to doing this. As of this writing, you will be required to enroll in TRICARE

Prime if you want it. Tricare Standard enrollment is automatic. In 2018, TRICARE Standard will be renamed to TRICARE Select[11].

You'll also get to do one other thing you've never done before… pay for your health insurance. Starting in 2020, you'll need to pay a premium for TRICARE Select. The premium will start at $300 per year if you have dependents and $150 per year for a single retiree/survivor. Also in 2020, the annual catastrophic cap[12] will increase to $3,500 per year. Both of these amounts will increase in line with inflation. If you select TRICARE Prime, your annual premium will be $282.60 if you are single and $565.20 if you are married or have a family. Upon reaching Medicare eligibility age, you will transition to TRICARE For Life (TFL)[13], the premium will go away and the catastrophic cap will revert to $3,000.

Don't Get Double Taxed and Don't Leave Money on the Table

There is a potential "gotcha" the year you retire, and it involves the Thrift Savings Plan (TSP) and your potential 401(k)/403(b). You are allowed to contribute $18,000 (plus $6,000 if age 50 or older) to 401(k)/403(b)/TSP regardless of how many accounts and jobs you have[14]. This can present a couple of problems.

The first problem involves over-contributions. As mentioned, there is a limit on the amount you can contribute to these accounts. And if you have one employer for the entire year, then your employer will protect you from yourself. Even if you try to contribute more

---

11 Original guidance stated that you would be required to sign up for TRI-CARE Standard/Select. Recent guidance from the Defense Health Agency indicates that those enrolled in TRICARE Standard will automatically be enrolled in TRICARE Select.

12 The catastrophic cap is the maximum you will have to pay out of pocket for covered medical care.

13 TFL is covered in the "Far Rocks" chapter.

14 2017 numbers

than your annual limit, your employer should stop your contributions. This won't be true if you have more than one employer during a year, as one employer doesn't know what you deferred while working for another (including previous) employer. You'll have to watch the limit yourself. You'll want to do this, because things gets real bad on the tax front if you over-contribute. If you contribute more than your limit during a year, you must try to reverse the excess contributions before you file your tax return. I say "try" because your employer is not required to reverse the contributions. If this occurs, then the excess contributions will be subject to taxation in the year of contribution and will be taxed again when you withdraw them from your 401(k)/403(b)/TSP in retirement. Not good.

The second problem has to do with employer matching and will require you to predict the future to an extent. Many employers match a certain portion of your 401(k)/403(b)/TSP contributions. The matching percentage can be significant. If you contribute a significant amount to TSP before you retire, you might inadvertently limit the matching funds you can receive from your new employer in the year you retire. If you have a pretty good idea on what your job will be after you retire and how much contribution your employer will match, then be sure to leave yourself "headspace" to contribute at least as much as your employer will match while staying below the annual deferral limit.

Job Hunting Expenses

You might be able to deduct your job hunting expenses. As you make your transition you'll need to keep track of your expenses. When are job hunting expenses deductible? It is probably easier to say when they are _not_ deductible. They are _not_ deductible if:

- You are looking for a job in a new occupation.
- There was a substantial break between jobs.
- You are looking for a job for the first time.

You're actually not required to find a job to deduct your expenses. Deductible expenses include:

- Employment and outplacement agency fees.
- Preparation and mailing of resumes.
- Travel to an area to look for a job (if job hunting is the primary purpose of the travel).

Note that job hunting expenses do not include your interview suit or other personal wardrobe expenses[15]. It also doesn't include teeth whitening or other grooming expenses.

You might or might not be able to deduct any education you undertake to support your transition. In general, if the education is to meet a minimum education requirement of your present trade or will qualify you for a new trade or business, the expense is _not_ deductible. Conversely, if the education will improve your skills in your current trade, the education is deductible. The question becomes what is your present trade? As an example, if you are a program manager then a Project Management Professional (PMP) certification might be deductible as it improves skills in your current trade. Ultimately it will depend on the exact facts and circumstance of your particular situation.

One last thing to be aware of: These deductions will be itemized on Schedule A as miscellaneous deductions and will be subject to the 2% AGI floor. But, more importantly, miscellaneous deductions are added back to your income when calculating the Alternative Minimum Tax (AMT). Depending on your income, the size of your family, and how much you pay in state income tax, you might be subject to the AMT. More on the AMT later.

---

15 Those of you who go to the airlines may be able to deduct the cost of your airline uniforms.

State Income Tax Withholding

You may have heard there is this mysterious thing out there called *state income tax*. For whatever reason, DFAS will not automatically start withholding state income tax from your retirement pay. *You have to be proactive and tell them to start the withholding.* You should be able to do this when you're out-processing. Let me say that again. You have to be proactive. If you don't get this done before you retire, you can go into MyPay after you are officially retired and start the state income tax withholding.

Speaking of state income taxes, only your military pay is covered under the Servicemembers Civil Relief Act. This means that while you are on terminal leave, your military pay will continue to be taxable, or tax-free based on your state of residence claimed on your LES (leave and earnings statement). If you start work while on terminal leave however, that income will be "sourced" to whatever state you are working in and will be non-resident taxable income for the period you are on terminal leave. In other words, you'll have to pay taxes on it.

What Should I Do With All my Old Rental Properties?

A lot of senior military members collect rental real estate throughout their career. If this applies to you, there are a lot of things, on the tax front, you should consider before you put those houses up on the market. Let's talk about a couple of different scenarios...

Using the Primary Residence Exclusion

You might be able to exclude a portion of your gains when you sell your rental property. If you can claim the property as your primary residence, you can exclude up to $250,000 ($500,000 if a qualifying married couple) of capital gains from your taxable income. But, it isn't quite that simple. Regardless of whether the property qualifies as your primary residence you will still owe taxes on what are technically called 1250 gains. These gains are commonly called depreciation recapture and are due on the depreciation you took, or should have taken (assuming you sell the house for more than your original basis). We'll come back to that. How do you qualify for the primary residence exclusion?

There are criteria you must meet to qualify for the exclusion and there are special rules for military members. To qualify for the exclusion, you must own and use the home for your principal residence for at least 2 years during the 5-year period prior to selling it. The use and ownership test periods do not have to be concurrent. It gets a little tricky for married couples. To qualify for the increased exclusion, one spouse can meet the ownership test, but both spouses must meet the 2-year use test to claim the greater $500,000 exclusion. There are special rules for divorced spouses and in the case where one spouse is deceased.

If you moved out of the home incident to military orders, you have the right to suspend the 5-year period for not more than 10 years during the time you are on active duty. So, theoretically, you could have lived in the house for 2 of the 15 years prior to selling the house, if everything lines up perfectly[16].

If you're reading this book, there is a pretty good chance your time on active duty is about to end. The Internal Revenue Code is not particularly clear in this regard but I believe the suspension ends effective your retirement date. Back to 1250 gains...

When you rent out your property, you are required to depreciate the property in accordance with the Internal Revenue Code. At the very basic level, you will depreciate the lower of (1) the fair market value of the structure as of the date of placing it on

---

16 You live in the house for 2 years, suspend due to PCS orders for 10 years, making a total of 12 years. The clock starts again and you continue to rent the property for 3 years, for a total ownership time of 15 years. For purposes of the residency test, you have effectively lived in the house 2 of the previous 5 years.

the market for rent, or (2) the purchase price[17]. You are required to depreciate the real estate over 27.5 years, the IRS-determined useful life of the property. In theory, depreciation represents the reduction in value of the asset as time passes. The reality with real estate is that in most, but not all cases, the value of the real estate increases over time.

When you sell the property, the IRS basically says the reduction in value was inaccurate and therefore you must give the government back the money you received in refunds due to the depreciation you took. Officially, these are 1250 gains. One small bit of good news, under current tax law, 1250 gains are taxed at a maximum of 25%. There is a chance the depreciation-sheltered income you received would have been taxed at a rate greater than 25%.

One last point concerning rental properties. If you are a landlord and haven't experienced this yet, you'll find out you can only deduct losses on rental real estate against current income if your AGI is less than $150,000[18]. If your AGI exceeds the threshold, then your losses are suspended. The good news is when you sell the property, you can use the suspended losses to offset gains on the sale.

Watch Out for Non-Qualified Use

Non-qualified use is a period of time when the capital gain on your primary residence, as defined above, allocated to that time is not excluded from income. Non-qualified use only applies for time periods after 2008 and essentially is any time neither you nor your spouse uses the home as a principal residence. There are exceptions when absence will not be considered non-qualified use.

---

17 For depreciation purposes, you only depreciate the value of the structures and do not include the value of the land.

18 If your AGI exceeds $100,000, your deduction might be limited.

- First, if the time you or your spouse didn't occupy the house during the 5-year ownership and use test is _after_ the last date you or your spouse used the home as a principal residence, it is not considered non-qualified use. In other words, if you meet the 5-year ownership and use test, and you didn't move out and back into your house, you're okay.
- Second, up to 10 years during which the taxpayer or spouse was not living in the house due to military orders[19].
- Third, temporary absence due to change in employment, health or unforeseen circumstances.

If there is a period of non-qualified use, then you must prorate the gain. For instance, if you owned the home for 10 years and had 2 years of non-qualified use, 20% of the gains (not attributable to depreciation recapture) would be included in income. These gains will be taxed like other capital gain income.

Use a 1031 Exchange to Defer Taxes

If you're interested in staying in the rental business, but don't necessarily want to keep your current rental, you can accomplish what is called a 1031 exchange. These exchanges are also known as Like-kind Exchanges. If a 1031 exchange is conducted properly, the taxes on the gains associated with the transfer of the property are deferred. In its purest form, a 1031 is a barter transaction, but most 1031 exchanges are not conducted as such. By following a very specific and unforgiving set of steps, you can sell a property and buy a new one and still defer the gain.

The first rule is the property must be like-kind. Real estate for real estate is a like-kind exchange. For example you could exchange

---

19 The PCS must be at least 50 miles from the principal residence or you must be ordered to government quarters. The same exemption exists for members of the Foreign Service, or the intelligence community, or reservists.

a single family residence for a duplex. The second rule is you can never touch the money. Your transaction must be accomplished with the assistance of a qualified intermediary. It is important that all paperwork be completed to recognize the qualified intermediary as the party to the sale[20].

The next two rules could be a little trickier. First, you must identify the replacement property within 45 days of the sale of the initial property. Normally, you can identify up to three possible replacements. You must close on the new property, selected from one of the three previously identified replacements, within 180 days of the closing of the sale of the initial property.

You need to watch the dollars too. If you receive any cash or if your mortgage on the new property is less than on the original property, then you will have "boot." Boot is income that is taxable in the year of the sale. To avoid this, as a general rule of thumb, make sure the replacement property is more expensive than the property you sold and your mortgage is at least as large as your previous mortgage, but not so big that the cash you received on the sale of the first house is more than you need when closing on the second house.

One other point concerning a 1031 exchange. To complete a 1031 exchange you must have the intent to make the new property a rental. You must also make an effort to rent the property. To be totally in the clear, you should rent the property. After that, things get a little fuzzy. There is nothing that says that at some point in the future you can't change your mind. So, if you do an exchange into a rental property at the beach, at some point in the future you can make it _your_ beach house. Now, if you sell the house you'll have a pretty complicated tax problem, but you will have deferred the taxes on the prior sale until you sell the beach house. If you hold the beach property until you (and your spouse if applicable) pass

---

20 A competent real estate agent/broker and/or a qualified intermediary should be able to make sure this happens correctly.

away, then the basis of the house will "step-up" and the deferred taxes will go away. Let me explain what that means. On the later of your or your spouse's death (assuming you are married) the basis of the house will "step-up" to the fair market value of the house on the date of death. The 1250 gains will all go away and whoever inherits the house will be able to sell it with no taxes due on appreciation and the 1250 gains accumulated prior to the last death.

Take Terminal Leave or Sell It Back?

I occasionally get a question about whether it is "better" to sell back leave or take terminal leave. I know people talked about it when I was on active duty. I think it is a question that gets over-thought.

For one thing, I'm not sure financial considerations should be the determining factor on whether you should take terminal leave or not. You might actually want to take the pack off for a few weeks or months, and you might actually enjoy it. But if financial considerations are your primary driver, then here are some thoughts.

Most of us will set our retirement date before we have a start date established for a new job. In fact, many of us won't have a date to start at our new job before we've actually retired. In this situation, we know one thing. Once you set your retirement date, you'll receive full pay and allowances until your retirement date... regardless. If you don't have a job start date prior to your retirement date and you want to max out the money in your pocket, then keep working, receive your full pay and allowances until your retirement date and sell back your leave. If you land a job that starts prior to your retirement date and, as in the previous scenario, your goal is to put the most money possible into your pocket, start terminal leave the day you start at your new job and sell back any leftover leave.

If you are one of the fortunate few who have a firm job offer and start date prior to setting your retirement date, then you will maximize the amount of money in your pocket by setting a retirement date that will allow you to start terminal leave the day you start at the new job. Like I said though, putting the most money in your pocket might not be the most important factor when determining when to set your retirement date.

Before you're done in the military, there is one more thing you need to take care of.

Complete Your Budget

As I'm pretty sure you're aware, the United States Congress has a hard time completing their Constitutionally mandated requirement to pass a budget. That hasn't stopped them from saying that *you* must complete a budget and present it to your service designated organization prior to your retirement.

But, I don't want you to do a budget. I want you to do a spending plan. Budgets make us sad. Spending plans make us happy. Of course, you can call this whatever you want. I recommend you structure your spending plan by summing all of your income, and then subtracting the total of your expenses.

- Income:
  o Military retirement.
  o VA Disability Benefits.
  o Income from new employment.
- Expenses:
  o Taxes.
  o Insurance.
  o Investments.
  o Essential expenses.
  o Optional expenses.

The last two expenses, essential and optional expenses, can be used to help you determine how much life or disability insurance you need or how much investment income you'll need in retirement to have an acceptable standard of living. If you do this, your spending plan becomes a decision tool versus a control mechanism.

Those are the things you need to consider taking care of now–besides figuring out how big a shadow box you want and how much money you're going to put on the bar for your retirement party.

So, what is lurking out there in the future?

CHAPTER 3

FAR ROCKS

As explained in the previous chapter, there are a lot of things you need to take care of right away as you make the transition to civilian life, and they will consume a lot of your time. But there are some things out there on the horizon you want to keep your eye on too. The first one, hopefully, is way out there on the horizon. Your estate.

Estate Planning

Estate planning is no fun. Nobody wants to build an estate plan. In fact, I suspect some of you will skip this section because you're never going to die. That's fine. But before you do, please read the portion on Estate Organization. Then you can skip to the fun stuff.

Estate Organization

I'm a bit of a zealot about this, both from a professional standpoint and from the standpoint of an individual who has dealt with an estate. One of the most caring things you can do for your loved ones is to have your estate in "order." When someone needs to take care of you or settle your estate, he/she needs to be able to _find_ things. You owe it to your family to leave instructions and information for them. As a minimum these should include:

- Location of your original will.
- Location of the original or copies of your Powers of Attorney, Medical Directives and Trust Documents (you can also provide appropriate individuals copies of these documents).
- A list of financial accounts.
- A list of liabilities and bills that need to be paid.
- A list of automatic payments that need to be stopped.
- Location of the original or copies of your life insurance policies and their value.
- How to notify the Office of Personnel Management (OPM) and the VA in the event of your passing.
- Other items as you deem necessary:
  o Desires for your final arrangements.
  o Instructions for you pets.

You can organize your estate with a good old-fashioned three-ring binder, or you can choose a computer-based solution such as everplans™[21].

Planning for Your Estate

Everyone has an estate plan, even if they do nothing. If you do no estate planning, the state will do it for you. Your estate will be distributed in accordance with the estate law in the state where you live (in most cases). I don't know about you, but that scares me. Since I, and hopefully you, don't want the state deciding what happens to your "stuff," I think estate planning is a pretty good idea. So let's start with some basics. But before I do let me say one thing:

Hire a pro!

---

[21] You can learn more about everplans™ at https://www.everplans.com/.

This is not something you should do yourself on Legal Zoom or some other on-line site. You also shouldn't buy a boiler plate will at Office Depot. And, as much as I love my JAG brethren, you are at a point in your life where the Base/Post Legal Office is not the appropriate place to complete your estate plan. Okay, on to the basics.

You have several estates. To start with, your estate is pretty much everything you own. In estate planning, this is called your "gross estate." It includes all your tangible assets (your stuff), your intangible assets (your investments), and some things you may not be thinking about such as the actuarial value of your Survivor's Benefit Plan or the value of your life insurance policy's death benefit (if you own the policy).

The "next" estate is your probate estate. Your probate estate is everything that is controlled by your will and, in most cases, is owned solely by you[22]. So if your will says, "Give all my tangible and intangible assets to my spouse," then essentially everything will go to your spouse.

Probably, what is equally important is what is not controlled by your will, and therefore is not included in your probate estate. Some of the big ones are:

- Life insurance proceeds (unless you name your estate as your beneficiary).
- Proceeds from retirement accounts.
- Joint accounts (in many cases).
- Annuities.

It is also important to note that a lot of you could have more than one probate estate. How can that be? If you have collected real estate around the country, you will have probate estates in the state

---

22 Certain types of joint ownership do not transfer by contract but are instead controlled by the decedent's will.

where you are a resident plus, potentially, the states where you own real estate. So if you have an "impressive" rental property collection, you could be subject to the probate process in several states. And with probate comes the expenditure of time and resources.

The final estate I'll talk about is your taxable estate. Your taxable estate starts out as your gross estate. We then deduct several things from it to arrive at your taxable estate. Those deductions include any liabilities of the estate, any expenses of the estate, and any charitable contributions made by the estate. There is also an unlimited tax deduction for any assets given to your spouse (such as the actuarial value of SBP). This value (gross estate minus deductions) will provide the basis for your estate tax. There is one other step in calculating your tax due. You have a lifetime unified credit, which shields $5.49 million[23] of your estate from taxation. Married couples can "share" their credit so it is possible to transfer nearly $11 million without estate tax ramifications. The amount shielded by the credit is reduced by any _taxable_ gifts you may have given during your lifetime. For reference, taxable gifts are:

- Gifts that exceed the annual exclusion amount, which is currently $14,000, to any individual or trust.
- Gifts that are not a gift of a "present interest." A gift of a present interest is one that the person who receives the gift can use without any restrictions/time limitations.

While Federal Estate Taxation is a concern for a small minority of Americans, the same is not necessarily true at the state level. Many states also levy estate taxes, and some levy inheritance taxes. Estate and/or inheritance tax might be a determining factor when you decide where to live for your "final" retirement. First what is the difference between the two? Estate taxes are levied on the value of the estate and paid by the estate. Inheritance taxes are levied

---

23 In 2017. Exclusion is indexed to inflation.

based on who receives the money and how much they receive. Technically, the person who inherits the money owes the tax, but many states require that the executor of the estate withhold the tax prior to paying the heir.

Fifteen states[24] and the District of Columbia tax estates. Some states tie their estate tax threshold to the Federal estate tax level. Some do not, and at the low end, New Jersey taxes estates that exceed \$675,000[25]. Six states[26] have an inheritance tax, and who pays and the rate the heirs pay varies widely.

Planning Considerations

Probate, taxes, and transferring ownership can cost money...a lot of money if you don't plan carefully.

Probate Avoidance

The probate process takes time and costs money. A well-crafted estate plan can avoid probate if that is an objective. Techniques to avoid probate include:

- Placing assets (especially real estate located in another state) inside a properly constructed trust to remove them from your probate estate. The trusts that accomplish this are known by different names, but some of the most common are Living Trusts, Revocable Trusts, or Grantor Trusts (or perhaps a combination of all three). These trusts do

---

24 States with an estate tax are: Connecticut, Delaware, Hawaii, Illinois, Maine, Maryland, Massachusetts, Minnesota, New Jersey, New York, Oklahoma, Oregon, Rhode Island, Tennessee, Vermont, and Washington.

25 New Jersey recently passed legislation that will eliminate the estate tax there in 2018.

26 States with an inheritance tax are: Nebraska, Iowa, Kentucky, Pennsylvania, plus Maryland and New Jersey, which also have an estate tax.

not reduce your estate tax liability, and they have no effect on your income tax.

- Changing your asset/account type to Transfer on Death (TOD) or Payable on Death (POD) will also remove the asset from your probate estate. With a TOD/POD designation, you are telling the financial institution or the government that upon your death you want the asset(s) to transfer to someone or to a trust. This designation supersedes your will and the assets transfer outside your probate estate. Joint accounts (for instance, accounts held jointly with your spouse) can also be TOD/POD, and the assets will transfer when the second account owner dies. In some states (Virginia is one example), real estate can be deeded as TOD.

- Joint accounts can be an option to avoid probate, but be very careful. If, for example, you name Junior as a joint account owner on your bank account, depending on the exact type of joint ownership you choose, the account will transfer outside probate when you pass. There are two very important warnings with this arrangement though. First, if Junior runs his car into a busload of nuns and gets sued, _your_ joint bank account could be taken as part of the settlement. Second, if you use a will as your primary estate planning tool and Junior is only on your account as a convenience, your estate may not convey as you desire. Let's say you want everything split equally between your two children. Junior is a joint owner (with rights of survivorship) of your $100,000 CD. When you pass, 100% of your CD will go to Junior, regardless of what your will says. Your daughter has no legal claim to the money, and Junior can keep it all. Even if Junior is a good "kid," knows what you wanted, and decides to give one-half to his sister, all is not well. The amount Junior gives to his sister is considered a gift and the gift tax kicks in; $36,000 ($50,000 - $14,000 annual exclusion) of the gift will be subject to gift tax. Junior will have to file a Gift Tax Return (Form 709). Most likely Junior won't owe any tax, but he will use up $36,000 of his lifetime exclusion.

- Make sure you don't make the situation worse. If you name your estate as the beneficiary of your life insurance, you just moved your life insurance proceeds *into* your probate estate. The same thing applies for your retirement plans (TSP, 401(k), IRAs). On a related note, I've heard anecdotally that several personnel agencies (MSS/MPF as an example) recommend designating "By Law" on your SGLI beneficiary designation. This could put your SGLI proceeds into your probate estate as well.

- If you own rental real estate outside of your state of residence and only want to eliminate probate in *that* state, you could consider transferring ownership of the real estate to a business entity, such as a Limited Liability Company (LLC). If you do this, when you pass, the company may go through probate in your state of residence rather than the real estate going through probate in the state of its location. This step also helps protect your other assets if you are sued because of something that happens at the rental.

Estate Tax Avoidance

At the Federal level, under current law, most of us will not owe estate tax. As mentioned previously, many of us might be subject to estate tax at the state level. But since "dead men don't vote" (except in Chicago), I anticipate this is one place the Federal Government could look to raise revenue, most likely through a lower estate tax threshold. Oh, and one other thing....some of you will find yourself subject to the Federal Estate Tax even if it doesn't come down. You'll be that successful. If either of these scenarios becomes a reality for you, there are things you can do to you lower your potential estate tax.

Transfer Ownership of Your Life Insurance Policies. Life insurance proceeds are included as a part of your taxable estate *if* you own the policy. You have the right/ability to transfer ownership of your life insurance policy. There are a few limitations though…

- *The Transfer Is a Gift.* If you transfer ownership to your spouse, there are no gift tax ramifications. If you transfer to someone else (Junior as an example) the transfer could be taxable. If the present value of the policy is more than $14,000, then the excess amount is subject to gift tax. However, the present value will be less than the face value of the policy, so you'll use less of your lifetime unified credit. You can also transfer the life insurance to an Irrevocable Trust, commonly called an ILIT, and accomplish the same thing.

- *Beware the "Insurance Triangle."* In an insurance policy there are three parties…the owner, the beneficiary, and the insured. There can be only two people in those three positions. In other words both the owner and insured need to be the same person or the owner and beneficiary need to be the same person. If not, when the insured dies, it is assumed the owner made a taxable gift to the beneficiary of the face value of the policy.

Make Gifts Below the Annual Exclusion. As mentioned, you can make a gift of up to $14,000 to anyone with no gift tax ramifications (as long as the gift is a gift of a present interest[27]). Your

---

27 To be a gift of a present interest, the person who receives the gift must be able to use it immediately. This means most gifts to trusts are not a gift of a present interest. However, if the trust has "Crummy Powers," then the gift may still qualify as a gift of a present interest.

spouse can do the same. So as a couple you can gift $28,000 to an individual. This can add up quickly. Let's say Junior is married and has two children. You and your spouse could gift $112,000 to that family each and every year with no gift tax liability.

Make Gifts Not Subject to the Annual Exclusion Limit. If you pay for tuition (not all qualified education expenses) directly to a qualified domestic or foreign institution there is no limit to the amount that can be gifted without gift tax ramifications. The same generally holds true for medical expenses. Funds paid directly to an institution that provides medical care or to a company that provides medical insurance are not subject to gift tax limitations. Generally speaking, if the medical expense is deductible as an itemized deduction this rule applies. Just to say it one more time, in both these cases, the payment must be made to the institution and not to an individual. This is why when you paid for Junior's college (directly to the institution) there weren't any gift tax ramifications.

Make Gifts Over the Annual Exclusion. It may make sense to get rapidly appreciating assets or assets you expect to appreciate in the future out of your estate[28]. Similar to gifting life insurance, you may use up part of your lifetime unified credit, but you will use less of it. Also, the person who receives your gift might be able to sell it and pay zero capital gains tax (if in the 10% or 15% tax bracket, under current law).

Contribute to 529 Plans. If you have grandchildren you might want to consider contributing to a 529 plan you own, but name the grandchild as the beneficiary. Although a gift to a 529 is _not_ a gift of a present interest, there is a special carve-out in the law that allows you to treat the contributions as a gift of present interest.

---

28 This is not always the best choice. In some circumstances it may make more sense to pay the estate tax to obtain the "step-up" in basis for the asset. This is a relatively complex decision and you should seek professional advice prior to making it.

Additionally, you can treat a contribution of up to $70,000 as five $14,000 gifts for the next 5 years, and you won't go over the annual exclusion limit. But, you can't contribute again without gift tax ramifications for 5 years. As an additional benefit, in many states if you contribute to the state's sponsored 529 plan, you will receive a state income tax deduction (there might be limits to the annual amount...some states allow you to carry unused deductions forward).

Take Advantage of "Portability." It used to be that your lifetime unified credit died with you. That is no longer the case. Now you (more correctly your estate) can transfer your unused credit to your spouse. But the transfer is not automatic. Even if it isn't required because of the size of your estate (less than $5.49 million) you must file an Estate Tax Return, Form 706, and indicate you want to transfer your unused credit to your spouse. If you don't, the credit dies with you. For example, you and your spouse have an $8M estate owned separately 50/50 (you each individually own $4M in assets). Under your estate plan, your $4 million estate goes to your children. You have no requirement to file an Estate Tax Return. Your executor, being a smart fellow, decides to file a Form 706 and transfers your unused $1.49 million credit to your spouse. When your spouse passes, his or her estate has grown to $6 million. Since your executor elected to transfer the unused credit to your spouse, the $6 million transfers free of estate tax. If the election had not been made, the estate would owe approximately $174,000 in estate taxes. A pretty good return for filling out some paperwork.

Consider Charitable Giving. There are several planning techniques that allow you to make a charitable gift, remove assets from your estate, reduce your current income tax, and support a charity for many years to come. Here are a few examples:

Donor Advised Funds. I like to call a Donor Advised Fund (DAF) the "poor man's foundation." A DAF is a 501(c)3 charity in and of itself. What makes it different from other charities is that it holds funds/assets for years that you can then direct to other charities. For example, you have a large stock position in XYZ Corporation that has $10,000 in capital gains and a total value of $15,000. You've held the stock for over a year (most likely for decades). You decide to transfer the stock to a DAF, which qualifies you for a $15,000 tax deduction in the current year (note the deduction is limited to 30% of your AGI). Going forward you can direct a portion of the balance of your DAF to a charity of your choice. There are two caveats though. As the name implies, the donor (you) advises on where the proceeds of the fund go. Generally speaking, as long as you direct the funds to a qualified charity versus your cousin Vinny you shouldn't have any problem. The second caveat is you are expected to eventually make distributions. You can allow the assets to grow for a while and once you start distributions a distribution of 5% annually should be sufficient. And, of course, once you contribute the funds to the DAF, they're no longer yours and you can't get them back.

Charitable Remainder Trusts. CRATs (Charitable Remainder Annuity Trusts) and CRUTs (Charitable Remainder UniTrusts) provide you, the donor, with an income stream and any money left over when you die goes to your designated charity. The difference between the two is a CRAT pays out a constant benefit and a CRUT pays out a varying amount based on the changing value of the principal in the trust[29]. Any assets moved to the trust are removed from your estate, provide for a current income tax deduction based on the present value of the remainder of the trust[30], and transfer capital gains on the assets to the charity, which means you will not pay taxes on those gains. These trusts are complicated and you definitely want to make sure you get competent legal advice to design them.

Charitable Lead Trusts. CLATs (Charitable Lead Annuity Trusts) and CLUTs (Charitable Lead UniTrusts) work just the opposite.

---

29 A portion of the payment from either a CRAT or a CRUT could be taxable.
30 The "remainder of the trust" is the actuarially calculated estimated value that will be left in the trust when you pass away.

The charity receives a stream of income from your contribution and a non-charity individual receives the remainder value. The tax ramifications of a CLT are a little more complicated than a Charitable Remainder Trust. There most likely will be a tax deduction for the value of the income stream to the charity but the deduction could accrue to you or to the trust depending on how the trust is set up. The remainder value of the trust could be subject to gift tax, depending on how the payout is made. Regardless, you will remove the entire value of the contribution from your taxable estate, and it is reasonable to assume the amount potentially subject to gift tax will be less than the amount subject to estate tax if you don't make the gift. Like remainder trusts, you will need qualified legal advice before executing this strategy.

Your Digital Estate

Planning for digital estates is a rapidly changing area of the law and much will change in the near future. When you develop an estate plan with your attorney you should discuss your digital estate. Some things to be aware of are:

- You don't own your Apple iTunes library like you used to own your "record albums." When you buy a song from Apple you buy a lifetime license to listen to the music. The right to listen to the music dies when you die. Many other digital products you buy, such as digital editions of books, are subject to the same limitation

- Depending on your instructions, when you pass away your accounts on sites like Facebook could be shut down and your heirs might not have access to the account.

- Violation of the terms of agreement of a website, logging in on someone else's account even with permission as one example, can be a crime.

Estate Planning Summary

I hope you don't have to execute your estate plan for many, many years. But the reality is someone will need to take care of your affairs at some point in the future. It is a whole lot easier, from both a capacity and an emotional standpoint, to get a plan together in your 50s than in your 70s...or even later. As you settle into a new job and potentially a new state, it is time to put your affairs in order.

Long-Term Care

I can't speak for you, but when I was on active duty I was invincible. Now that I qualify for the Senior Citizen Discount at McDonalds, my opinion is starting to "evolve." As much as we'd all like to believe we will age without diminishing capacity, the reality is, at some point we'll probably need some help and that help will come in the form of long-term care.

Let's start with a quick definition of long-term care. First, it isn't medical care. What it is, is care that helps with your normal daily activities, such as getting up and around. You may get long-term care from your spouse, your children, or a professional. If you need professional help, that help will have to be paid for.

It is important to know that Medicare and TRICARE _do not_ pay for long-term care[31]. Medicaid does pay for long-term care, but to qualify for Medicaid you have to spend down your assets and give up most of your income. In general, to qualify for Medicaid you'll have to spend down assets to about $2,000 and you'll only be able to keep a very small amount of your pension and Social Security. That means unless you are willing to impoverish yourself

---

31 Under very specific circumstances, skilled nursing care, which looks a lot like long-term care will be covered. The time period is relatively short and you must be hospitalized prior to the care.

(and potentially your spouse) to qualify for Medicaid you need to come up with another solution.

How much money are we talking about? It varies greatly, depending on where you live. Therefore, long-term care costs might be a determining factor when deciding where to "retire, retire." The current national averages[32] are shown in Table 3.

Table 3: 2017 National Averages for Long-Term Care

Type of Care	Unit Cost	Annual Cost
Nursing home, semiprivate room	$277/day	$82,855
Assisted living facility	$3,427/month	$41,124
Home care	$19/hour	$29,640*

*Assumes 6 hrs/day, 5 days/week

I've always found it a little interesting that nursing home care costs are pretty darn close to the amount a retired O-6 receives in pension payments (pre-tax). Before you say to yourself, "Got it covered," remember you might not be the only one involved here, you still have to pay taxes, and you might want home care, which means you'll still have many of your other expenses.

Since we've identified government programs as an unlikely source of funding for long-term care, you'll need to either pay for this potential expense from your assets and income or transfer the risk via insurance. Insurance for long-term care is unimaginatively called Long-Term Care Insurance (LTCI). Now, before you say, "there is no way I'm buying insurance to pay for a nursing home," let me try to change your sight picture.

Individuals go into nursing homes for two reasons. The first reason is there is no way the appropriate care can be provided in the home. The second reason has to do with money. While home care seems to be less expensive than nursing home care, if you

---

32 According to the Federal Long-Term Care Website; http://www.ltcfeds. com/start/aboutltc_cost.html

or your spouse needs more than 15 hours of care per day, then the nursing home is less expensive. Or, put another way, could you absorb $82,000 per year in additional expenses and stay at home, indefinitely? LTCI is really "stay at home" insurance and I recommend you look at it that way. Nearly all senior citizens want to stay at home as long as possible. LTCI can help you reach that goal.

If you're going to purchase LTCI, you'll want to understand the basics of LTCI contracts. Here are a few:

- **Daily Benefit Amount.** The maximum amount the insurance policy will pay, per day.
- **Benefit Period.** This is the minimum amount of time, in years, the insurance policy will pay benefits. Common benefit periods are 3 and 5 years, but other options are available.
- **Maximum Lifetime Benefit.** This is total amount the policy will pay. It is determined by the multiplying the daily benefit amount by the benefit period in days.
- **Waiting/Elimination Period.** This is the plan's "deductible." It is the number of days you will have to pay your own way before the insurance policy starts to pay.
- **Inflation Protection.** If selected, inflation protection increases your daily benefit amount by a pre-selected inflation factor. The inflation protection generally is not based on the actual inflation rate of long-term care. Inflation protection can be compound or simple.

It is important to note that LTCI math isn't always like other math. When looking at policy options, it is important to understand the relationship between the daily benefit amount, benefit period, and maximum lifetime benefit. The best way to think of the relationship is the maximum lifetime benefit is a pool of money that can be spent no faster than the daily benefit amount per day. In other words, if you spend less than the daily benefit amount per day on your care, the benefit period will grow beyond the amount stated in the policy. This leads to a corollary that *if you are looking at trade-offs to control policy cost, it is better to shorten the benefit period and maintain a high daily benefit amount.*

When does LTCI pay out? LTCI normally pays when you or your spouse, if covered, are no longer able to accomplish two out of five Activities of Daily Living (ADLs) without assistance *or* have cognitive impairment. The ADLs are:

- Bathing.
- Dressing.
- Eating.
- Continence.
- Transferring (getting into or out of a chair or bed).

If these conditions become an issue, then a policyholder files a claim to start the clock running on the waiting/elimination period. Most likely, the insurance company will want to do its own verification of the condition during the elimination period. Once the condition is verified and the waiting period has passed, the policy will start paying benefits at a rate no faster than the daily benefit amount.

If you decide you want to transfer the risk of long-term care costs via insurance, you should do so sooner rather than later. This is due to a few different reasons. First, insurability may become an issue. In most cases, you will need to undergo a medical exam or at least complete a medical questionnaire as part of the underwriting process, and by delaying you could develop a condition that makes you uninsurable[33]. Second, if you delay, due to inflation you will need to purchase an increasing amount of insurance with less time to pay for it, so premiums will increase geometrically (very rap-

---

33 Conditions that make you uninsurable for life insurance might not make you uninsurable for LTCI and vice versa.

idly). Third, long-term care isn't just for "old people." Sometimes care is needed due to an accident or illness, and LTCI may provide support for you and take the load off of family members.

Where should you buy LTCI? You have a couple of choices, the Federal Long-Term Care Insurance Program (FLTCIP) and the "commercial" market.

As a military retiree you and your spouse have access to the FLTCIP[34]. Benefits of the FLTCIP include gender-neutral pricing and potentially relaxed underwriting. Recently, commercial insurers have started basing premiums on the gender of the insured. Because women tend to survive their spouse and are more likely to need long-term care, they pay more for a LTCI policy than men with the same characteristics would pay. This may make the FLTCIP more affordable for a couple or a single female. Also, since the FLTCIP is a group policy, it is possible underwriting standards will be relaxed as compared to an individual policy.

You also have the option to purchase LTCI on the commercial market, and there are some different benefits in commercially available policies. To me, the biggest benefit is that some plans can be designated as "partnership" plans. The availability of partnership plans varies from state to state. Partnership plans allow you to provide for your care, including using Medicaid benefits, and maintain an estate for your spouse or heirs. When covered by a LTCI policy that is a partnership plan, you are allowed to keep assets equal to the amount your LTCI policy paid for your care and still qualify for Medicaid. In other words, you don't have to spend down your assets to $2,000 or so[35] prior to starting Medicaid.

---

34 As mentioned in the SBP section, spouses are eligible if either the retired military member is receiving an annuity or the spouse is receiving a survivor's annuity. So, if you pass away and did not select SBP, your spouse will lose the ability to purchase insurance through the FLTCIP. If your spouse is female, she will almost certainly pay a much higher premium for the same level of coverage for a non-FLTCIP policy.

35 The exact amount varies by state.

Another option with commercially available policies is "shared benefits." Shared benefits are usually provided if you purchase a rider. If the rider is purchased, then a husband and wife can share their benefits. If one spouse doesn't use any or all of his or her benefits, the other spouse can.

There is one other option for LTCI if you have health conditions that prevent you from purchasing commercially available LTCI. There are hybrid life insurance policies and annuities that carry long-term care riders. Many times you can exchange an existing life insurance policy or annuity for a hybrid product that contains a long-term care benefit with different underwriting requirements than a pure LTCI policy.

Social Security

You have paid into Social Security for your entire career. You'll continue to pay into it if you are employed in the civilian sector. Currently, individuals pay social security taxes on up to $127,200 of earned income.[36] If you go down the path of starting your own business, you'll get to pay twice the "normal" Social Security Tax. This is because a self-employed individual pays both sides of the Social Security tax. For some reason, this tax isn't called FICA like for an employee, but is called self-employment tax. Since self-employment tax includes the "employer's portion" of Social Security taxes, self-employed individuals get to deduct ½ of self-employment tax from income. Hopefully that will make those of you who are self-employed happy.

After you're done paying into Social Security, you're going to want to get something out. In almost all circumstances, it makes sense to delay claiming Social Security for as long as possible, up to the age of 70. Why is that?

---

36 As of January 2017. Medicare taxes are paid on all earned income.

You've heard the first one before. Longevity risk. You know exactly how many years, days, hours, minutes, and seconds there are between now and the day you turn 70. You have no idea of how many years, days, hours, minutes, and seconds there are between the day you turn 70 and the day you die, or your spouse dies. Solving the income problem from today until you turn 70 is a much easier problem than solving the income problem from age 70 until death. Even if you have to spend down assets from age 62 to age 70, in most cases you will be better served by delaying claiming Social Security benefits. A few of the reasons are...

- **Benefits Are Significantly Higher.** Your benefits go up between 7% and 8% per year you delay claiming them. In other words, your benefits will be 76% higher, inflation adjusted, at age 70 versus age 62.[37]
- **Survivor Benefits.** If your spouse survives you, he or she will receive the greater of his or her Social Security benefit or yours.

You'll probably make more money, even though this isn't the main reason to delay claiming Social Security. Actuarially, regardless of when you claim benefits, you will receive the same amount if you die at the Social Security calculated life expectancy. But, the last time the Social Security Administration updated the life expectancy calculations, Ronald Reagan was President. Most likely, life expectancy has increased in the last 30 years. Beyond that, remember, if you are married, your benefits could continue beyond your death.

If both you and your spouse have enough earnings to qualify for Social Security individually, then you have more options. Until recently there were a whole lot of options. While the correct

---

37 Why it Pays to Delay Social Security Benefits, Money Magazine, http://time.com/money/3819584/delay-social-security-benefits/

option will depend on your specific situation, in general consider having the lower-earning spouse claim benefits at Full Retirement Age (FRA) and the higher earning spouse claim benefits at age 70. While not always the case, this will often provide the highest benefit for a surviving spouse, and it is likely to provide the greatest total income.

If you had children late in life, there might be one other option. Children of Social Security recipients receive benefits until they turn 18 or graduate from high school, whichever is later. If you're 62 or older and you have a child still in high school, you might want to consider claiming benefits until your child graduates from high school and then suspend your benefits until age 70. This could provide a pretty good windfall for funding your child's college education. However, if you're still working, the Wages/Social Security Benefits offset could make this option less appealing. Again, whether it makes sense for you will depend on your situation.

One thing you'll want to check on when you file for Social Security is whether your income records have been "grossed up." For most individuals who served in the military prior to 2001, the income used to calculate your Social Security benefits for the time you served will be increased.[38]. For those who served between 1968 and 2001, for every $300 in active duty basic pay, you will be credited with an additional $100 in earnings up to a maximum of $1,200 a year. According to the Social Security Administration, these credits will be automatically added to your record. However, in the words of one of my favorite Presidents, Ronald Reagan, "Trust but verify."

Social Security will be a major source of income for you and your spouse in retirement. Put some thought behind your claiming strategy and follow up on the details.

---

38 For more information, see https://www.ssa.gov/pubs/EN-05-10017.pdf

TRICARE

Your TRICARE coverage will continue when you retire, but as mentioned earlier, it will change. And, it will change significantly when you turn age 65.

When you turn 65 you will become eligible for Medicare. You will receive Part A coverage for "free," but let's face it, you've been paying for it for 45 plus years. Medicare Part A covers hospital care. You are eligible to select Medicare Part B, which covers doctors and non-hospital care (not everything is covered though). You will also have the option to purchase Medicare Part D, which is prescription drug coverage, but as of this writing, TRICARE prescription coverage is better than Medicare Part D.

When you sign up for Medicare Part B, you become eligible for TRICARE For Life (TFL). TFL is essentially Medicare Parts A and B combined with TRICARE Standard. If you need medical care covered both by Medicare and TRICARE, then Medicare will pay 80% of the covered care and TRICARE will pay the 20% co-pay. In other words, you won't have any out of pocket expenses for the medical care.

If you need medical care covered only by Medicare, then you will be responsible for the Medicare co-pay, which is normally 20% of the Medicare approved amount. *Please note, Medicare does not have a catastrophic cap.*

If you need medical care covered only by TRICARE, you will be responsible for the TRICARE co-pay, which is 20% until you reach your annual catastrophic cap of $3,000[39]. In other words, the maximum you will pay for TRICARE-only covered services is $3,000 per year.

You need to be aware of a couple of "gotchas" when it comes to TFL. Remember, *you have to take Medicare when you are eligible.* Your Medicare eligibility age has nothing to do with your Social Security eligibility age. Your Social Security FRA most likely is 67,

---

39 The increase in the TRICARE Select catastrophic cap does not apply to TFL.

but your Medicare eligibility age is still 65. So, you need to remember to sign up for Medicare when you turn 65.

You also need to watch out for HR departments that understand Medicare but not TFL. If you decide to work past age 65, you might be advised by your HR department that you don't need to take Medicare since you have credible coverage through your employer. This is true, but you'll lose TRICARE coverage[40], something you might not want to happen.

Second, if you decide to move overseas in retirement, you might be tempted to decline Medicare since Medicare generally does not cover overseas medical care. If you do, you'll also lose TRICARE coverage. To maintain TRICARE coverage while living overseas, you'll have to pay for Medicare Part B you can't use.

In certain situations (CSRS retirees or some state employees), your spouse might not be eligible for Medicare based on his or her earnings record. This might occur if your spouse is older than you and has reached age 65, and you have not. If this is the case, then you need to get documentation from the Social Security Administration that your spouse does not qualify for premium-free Medicare Part A. Then your spouse will be eligible to continue with his or her current TRICARE coverage until when/if he or she becomes eligible for Medicare under your record. You will have to spend some time at Pass and ID to update DEERS and get a new ID card for your spouse to maintain TRICARE coverage.

Thrift Savings Plan (TSP)

One thing you can take off your very full retirement/transition plate is deciding what to do with your TSP. You don't have to do anything with your TSP when you leave the military. In fact, you don't have to do anything with your TSP until you turn age 70 ½

---

40 You can reinstate your TRICARE coverage by signing up for Medicare in the future.

(hopefully, we can all remember to do "something" with it when we turn age 70 ½). There are a lot of good reasons to leave your money in TSP. Here are a few:

Phenomenally Low Expense Ratios. Expense ratios matter. In fact, according to Morningstar®, expense ratios are the single best indicator of future performance. TSP has expense ratios lower than any other option available.

The G Fund. If you want to hold a certain portion of your portfolio in cash, the G Fund could be an excellent choice. The G Fund is essentially a money market fund on steroids. The G Fund pays an interest rate based on a weighted average of medium to long-term government bond interest rates. Normally, to get medium to long-term interest rates you need to accept principal risk. Principal risk reflects the fact that as interest rates go up, bond prices tend to go down. The G Fund resets interest rates monthly, and as a practical matter, this eliminates principal risk. In theory you should never lose money in the G Fund, much like a Money Market Mutual Fund, but you get interest payments as if you could lose money.

Tax Exempt Balance. There is a pretty good chance you have a tax exempt balance in your TSP account. If this is the case, you can only transfer that balance to a fund/account that can account for the tax exempt balance. This might or might not be possible. If it isn't possible and you transfer funds out of TSP, your tax exempt balance will be paid out to you. You won't owe any taxes, but you'll lose any future tax-deferred earnings.

Future Required Minimum Distributions (RMD) "Control." If you continue to work for the Government and think you might work past age 70, then combining your military TSP with your civilian TSP could help you control your future RMDs. If you work for the Government, past 70 ½, you can delay taking your RMDs until you stop working[41]. If

---

41 This also applies if you work for a company where you aren't a 5% or greater owner, but you would use the company's 401(k) versus TSP.

you pull your traditional IRA balances and your military TSP balance into your Civil Service TSP, you can delay taking distributions from your IRAs too. However, if you do have a tax exempt balance in your military TSP, you can't transfer the tax exempt balance to the Civil Service TSP. I can't explain that...

There are also some pretty good reasons to take your money out of TSP. TSP, like any other investment "vessel," has some limits. You might want to roll your TSP into an IRA account for the following reasons:

- **Access to Additional Asset Classes.** While you can build an adequately diversified portfolio inside of TSP, there are asset classes you can't reach. For example, you can't invest in precious metals, real estate using Real Estate Investment Trusts, emerging markets, or international corporate bonds.
- **Distribution Flexibility.** Unfortunately, you don't have many options for withdrawal from your TSP. You are allowed two "partial" withdrawals. Your second withdrawal must be a full withdrawal unless you select one of the periodic payment options. Otherwise, you must do one of the following:
  - You can select a monthly dollar amount until your account runs out of money. The withdrawal amount can be changed annually.
  - You can also select monthly payments based on your IRS life expectancy.
  - Or you can purchase an annuity that will pay a set amount, possibly inflation adjusted, until you or your spouse pass away, depending on the type of annuity selected.
- **Distribution Control.** Additionally, your distributions come out proportionally by investment class and account type. In other words if your account is 50/50 Roth/Pre-Tax, then

your distribution will be 50/50 Roth/Pre-Tax. The same concept applies if your balance is 50/50 C/F Fund:

o Transferring your TSP balance to an IRA can give you the ability to manage your distributions to minimize taxes and Medicare premiums and to take out a large amount without limitations for a curveball life may throw at you.

- **Estate Planning Concerns.** When you pass, if your spouse is your beneficiary[42], your TSP account will pass to him/her, and a beneficiary account will be established. Your asset allocation will be disregarded and your balance will be 100% invested in the Lifecycle fund targeted most closely to the year your spouse turns 62. If a different asset allocation is desired, your spouse will need to change this.

If someone other than your spouse is designated as a beneficiary, then the balance of your TSP will be paid out directly, fully taxable, or to an inherited IRA(s), which would delay taxation. These limitations are not too bad. But the next branch and sequel gets pretty bad.

If your spouse inherits your TSP, leaves the funds in TSP, and then passes away, the entire balance of the beneficiary TSP account will be paid out to the new beneficiaries. It can't be rolled over to an inherited IRA. If there is a significant balance left in your TSP when your spouse passes away, then Junior will inherit the entire amount, and it will subject to taxation...in 1 year. This could push Junior into a higher tax bracket and give a greater cut to Uncle

---

42 If you don't designate beneficiaries via a Form TSP-3, your account will be distributed IAW Federal law, _not_ your will. The funds will be distributed to (in order): Your spouse; if none, your child or children equally; if none, to your parents equally; if none, to the executor of your estate; if none, to your next of kin who is entitled to your estate under the laws of the state in which you resided at the time of your death.

Sam. If, on the other hand, the TSP funds inherited by your spouse had been transferred to an IRA, or if you had originally transferred your TSP to an IRA, the final beneficiaries would be able to stretch the withdrawals out over a period of years and potentially reduce the total tax bill.

Participant Beware

After you retire, you have the option of taking a withdrawal from your TSP balance and redepositing it into an IRA within 60 days. Usually this occurs when a participant has a "plan" to use the money for a short period and then deposit the funds into the IRA. But things might not work out like that for you. Here is how things actually work. Let's say you have $100,000 in your TSP and you request a withdrawal to "roll-over" to an IRA. When the check shows up in the mail, it will be for $80,000. When you call TSP to ask what happened, the nice person on the TSP help line informs you they must withhold 20% in case you don't make the roll-over and taxes are due. You successfully complete your "plan" to use the money and deposit the $80,000 into a roll-over IRA 59 days later. When you file your taxes, you only receive a $13,000 refund. You call the friendly IRS help line to get an explanation and find out you were taxed on the $20,000 distribution you took (otherwise known as the taxes withheld) plus a 10% penalty because you're not age 59 ½ years old yet (($20,000 x 25%)+($20,000 x 10%) = $7,000) To avoid paying the taxes, you would have needed to find $20,000 from another source and contribute it to your IRA to make a total rollover of the $100,000 balance that was in your TSP. Oh and by the way, if your plan doesn't work and you roll over the funds 61 days after you took them out of your TSP, the entire distribution is subject to tax and penalty[43]. You can avoid all this by doing a Trustee-to-Trustee transfer; 100% of your balance

---

43 Under certain circumstances, the penalty can be waived.

will transfer, and you won't owe any taxes. But you have the right to do it yourself, and you have the right to mess it up. Don't.

Required Minimum Distributions (RMDs)

As I mentioned earlier, when you turn 70 ½ you'll have to do something with your TSP. That something is to take RMDs. And, RMDs don't just apply to TSP. They apply to 401(k)s, 403(b)s, IRAs and other retirement accounts as well. The one notable exception is Roth IRAs. As of this writing, RMDs are not required from Roth IRAs, but there is a move afoot to make RMDs a requirement for Roth IRAs. The administration claims this will "simplify" things. I think it is to increase tax revenue…but that's just me.

What is an RMD? As the name implies, it is a minimum amount you must take from your retirement account each and every year after you turn 70 ½. Let me clarify the whole 70 ½ thing though. Technically, you are required to begin taking your RMDs the year you turn 70 ½. This is called your required beginning date. The law does allow you to delay the distribution until 1 April the year after you turn 70 ½. I have to note, only Congress could come up with a rule like this. What many people don't realize is if they delay the first distribution until 1 April of the year after they turn 70 ½, then a second distribution, for the "current" year will be required prior to 31 Dec of the year after turning 70 ½. Complicated enough?

How much do you need to take out? The answer is based on two variables. The first variable is the account balance at the start of the year of the distribution. Technically, it is the balance of the account on 31 December of the year prior to the year of distribution. Since 1 January is a holiday the balance is the same on both days. The second variable is your life expectancy. You're probably thinking to yourself, "I don't know how long I will live." Not to worry, the IRS does. Your life expectancy is listed in an IRS Tax Table. You can find the tax tables at www.irs.gov. Most tax payers will use the Uniform Life Table[44]. For some reason, the IRS has a different life expectancy for those whose spouse is more than 10 years younger than the taxpayer. I'll leave it to you to determine why the life expectancy is different in the two different cases. The IRS, via the Uniform Life Table, says that at age 70, your life expectancy is another 27.4 years.

Once you determine your life expectancy, then you need only divide your account balance by the calculated life expectancy. For example if you are 70 and have a TSP balance of $500,000 your RMD is $18,248.18 ($500,000 ÷ 27.4). The next year, you would go back to the table to determine your life expectancy is now 26.5 years. The math remains the same.

Two bits of good news. Most investment custodians will do the calculations for you, so you won't need to. Second, at least according to the IRS, if you make it to 115 years of age, you will never die. The Uniform Life Table says all taxpayers age 115 and older have a 1.9-year life expectancy.

Where you take your RMDs from is a little complicated. If you have multiple accounts that comprise your IRA, perhaps at multiple mutual fund companies, you can aggregate your RMDs and take them from one account. The same does _not_ hold true for qualified accounts at your employer. If you have multiple 401(k)/403(b)/TSP accounts, you must take your RMDs from each account separately. And yes, you'll have to calculate the amount for each separate account.

While RMDs seem non-discretionary, there are planning opportunities. Just because you can wait until 70 ½ to start taking RMDs, that doesn't mean you should. If you have large balances in your retirement accounts, RMDs could put you into a higher tax bracket. You probably don't want that to happen. RMDs could also cause you to pay more for Medicare Part B. As mentioned in the Medicare section, you must pay premiums for Medicare Part B and

---

44 Table III in IRS Pub 590b.

you must have Medicare Part B to keep your TRICARE coverage. The amount you pay for Medicare Part B premiums is based on your income. If your AGI is greater than $170,000 (married filing jointly) or $85,000 (filing singly), you will pay more for Medicare Part B[45].

If you're concerned that once your RMDs start you'll be over the limit, you might want to take distributions prior to your required beginning date. The amount you take should fill up your current tax bracket, because you don't want to pay higher taxes than necessary on the withdrawal. You could take the money out and spend it on your lifestyle and preserve other assets. If you have other funds in a taxable account, using the taxable accounts for living expenses and converting the appropriate amount to a Roth IRA might make sense. This will allow you to leave money in a retirement account indefinitely, since RMDs are not required from Roth IRAs; if you do need the money later in life, the withdrawals will be tax free and will not affect your Medicare premiums.

But what if you don't need the money? There is only one way to postpone RMDs, and you must be working to do so. As previously mentioned, if you are still employed and your only retirement account is your current employer-provided plan, such as a 401(k)/403(b)/TSP, you are not required to take RMDs. To take advantage of this provision, you cannot be a 5%-or-more owner of the company. Also, if you have multiple retirement accounts, you'll need to transfer the funds into the qualified account prior

---

45 As of 2017, for taxpayers who file married filing jointly, the premiums and AGI breakpoints are: (1) Less than $170,000, the premium is $121.80 per month per person; (2) above $170,000 up to $214,000, the premium is $170.50 per month per person; (3) above $214,000 up to $320,000, the premium is $243.60 per month per person; (4) above $320,000 up to $428,000, the premium is $316.70 per month per person; and (5) finally for those with an AGI above $428,000, the premium is $389.80 per month per person. For those taxpayers who file single, then the premium brackets are cut in half; in other words, the first AGI breakpoint is $85,000 versus $170,000 (married filing jointly).

to being required to take RMDs, or you will have to take the RMD for any year you had a balance in your other retirement accounts.

If you chose to support charities, you have one other option. The IRS allows those who are required to take RMDs to transfer all or a portion of those RMDs directly to a qualified charity[46]. If you choose to do so, you don't take a charitable deduction, instead the amount transferred is not included in calculations of AGI. Since AGI controls several deductions and credits on your tax return, and your AGI also sets your Medicare premiums, this can be a very valuable tax planning opportunity. Another reason to consider this is as you progress into retirement you might lose the ability to deduct charitable contributions as you won't have enough deductions to itemize. *If you contribute directly from your IRA, you'll get the same benefit as a deduction, but without having to itemize.*

On a Related Note...

You need to be pretty aware when it comes to your RMDs from TSP (I love it when I can get that many acronyms in one sentence). As you already know, you must take your first RMD, including from TSP, by 1 Apr the year after you turn 70 ½. Things can get pretty weird if you don't instruct TSP to make your RMD or you don't withdraw enough to cover your RMD requirement. If you don't withdraw your required minimum distribution or instruct TSP prior to 1 Mar to make a required minimum distribution by the 1 Apr deadline, you will *forfeit* your TSP balance...calm down we'll get back to this. There is a bit of good news though, for the first year of RMDs, TSP will make a distribution on 1 Mar (prior to the required date) if they haven't already received instructions to make a distribution that meets the rules for required distributions, and you won't owe penalties to the IRS. But then you'll forfeit

---

46 The RMDs must be required due to age (i.e., 70 ½). You can t use this technique with an inherited IRA.

your balance. Once your TSP balance is forfeited, you will have the ability to get it back, but you will earn *zero* income on your balance during the time the funds are forfeited. To get your forfeited money back, you will need to file a form with TSP, and you will be required to make a full withdrawal. Fortunately, the withdrawal can be directed to an IRA so you won't have to pay taxes on the distribution, if you so choose.

One other point, unlike most 401(k)s and IRAs, you can't arrange for TSP to automatically pay out your RMD each year. You'll need to be taking periodic distributions, and if the distributions don't cover your RMD obligation, TSP will send an additional payment to cover your RMD.

CHAPTER 4

LEAD

You're about to have a new boss and "the man" might offer you a lot of things beyond your pay. Let's take a look at a few.

Civilian Retirement Plans

I have to admit it, when I went through the CFP® education program I found retirement plans to be the most difficult to understand. Why? I never had to pay attention to them during my career, unlike investments and taxes, which did affect me. I'm not going to teach you how to build a retirement plan, but when you are done with this section you should understand what your boss is offering you. Let's start with the basics. Qualified plans are the plans most of you will be offered, and they are covered next. Some of you will land positions that will offer non-qualified plans and those are covered later.

Qualified Plans

Qualified plans are generally offered to all employees or all employees of a specific class. Qualified plans must meet and satisfy several criteria and must be approved by the Department of Labor (DoL) and the IRS. Two significant criteria the plan must meet to be qualified are non-discrimination and vesting. In essence, the plan cannot discriminate in favor of highly compensated employees. Additionally, qualified plans must vest within a set timeframe.

Why do employers offer qualified plans? Beyond employee retention, employers can often gain greater tax benefits with a qualified plan than they do with a non-qualified plan.

Getting the Terms Right

One of the things that complicates understanding qualified retirement plans is the misuse of terms. Everyone from your parents to the "expert" in the unit to the financial magazine you read plays fast and loose with the terms used to describe retirement plans. Let's sort some of that out.

- **Pension.** When you hear the word *pension*, think mandatory. Your employer has a mandatory requirement to fund a pension plan. The funding must occur whether the company is profitable or not.
- **Profit Sharing.** When you hear the words *profit sharing*, think optional. Technically the contributions are not optional… the employer must make substantial and recurring contributions to the plan in order to maintain qualified status. But for our purposes, "optional" is close enough.
- **Defined Benefit.** With a defined benefit plan, the output is set by the plan document. You'll get "x" dollars per month for the remainder of your life, or a lump sum when you retire.
- **Defined Contribution.** In a defined contribution plan, what is put into the account is set by the plan document.

Actual retirement plans have a combination of these attributes, and there are four possible combinations that could result in a qualified retirement plan:

- **Defined Benefit Pension Plan.** These plans will often be described in terms such as these: "You will be paid 2½ percent times the number of years employed times the average of the highest 3 years of salary." (Sound familiar? If a military pension was a qualified plan, it would be a defined benefit pension plan.)
- **Defined Benefit Profit Sharing Plan.** They don't exist. Hard to get a set output with an optional input.
- **Defined Contribution Pension Plan.** In these types of plans, the employer will make a mandatory contribution each and every year, but will not set an output. It is common for these types of plans to pay a rate of return "pegged" to some index. These plans go by names such as *Cash Purchase* and *Target Benefit* plans.
- **Defined Contribution Profit Sharing Plan.** By the title, you know the employer makes substantial and recurring (optional) contributions, and there is no output defined. These plans are the most common. They typically involve a separate account in the employee's name where the employer deposits funds or securities on the employee's behalf. The most common of these plans is 401(k) matching[47].

Speaking of 401(k) matching, it is worth the time to discuss Safe Harbor matching. Just like other qualified plans, 401(k) plans cannot discriminate in favor of highly compensated employees. This can be a problem since 401(k) plan participation is voluntary. One way employers can avoid the problem of proving the plan does not discriminate is to select a Safe Harbor. If a plan makes contributions that meet Safe Harbor rules, the annual non-discrimination filing requirement is waived. A plan meets Safe Harbor rules if:

---

47 The contribution side of a 401(k) is technically a Cash or Deferred Arrangement (CODA) as the employee is deferring his/her salary into the account vice the employer contributing additional funds.

1. The employer contributes 3% of salary to all employees (whether they contribute or not), **OR**
2. The employer matches the first 3% of salary contributed by participants and 50% of the next 2%. As an example, under this Safe Harbor option, an employee who contributes 5% of salary to the 401(k) would receive a 4% match.

It is important to know whether your 401(k) is a Safe Harbor plan or not, because Safe Harbor contributions vest differently than Non Safe Harbor plans.

When Is the Money Mine?

The term for gaining the right to your money is *vesting*. When you vest is determined by the type of plan you are participating in. But before we look at that, there are different types of vesting. If the plan has cliff vesting, the employee will gain rights to 100% of his or her benefits at some point in the future. Under graduated vesting, the rights will be gained at a rate of 20% per year over a period of 5 years. In defined benefit plans, you may or may not be able to take money out immediately if you leave your job prior to retirement age. You will have the right to a future lump sum or payout over time. Defined contribution plans, on the other hand, do have a cash value you may have access to before retirement age. Back to the vesting schedule.

Employers can be more generous than the law requires, but to maintain qualified plan status the plan must vest in time to meet the following criteria:

- Defined benefit plans vest as follows:
  o 5-Year cliff vesting.
  o 3–7 Year graduated vesting (20% at 3 years, 40% at 4 years, etc.).
- Defined contribution plans vest under a different schedule:

- o   3-Year cliff vesting.
- o   2–6 Year graduated vesting.
- ▪ 401 (k) Plan asset vesting is a little more complicated:
  - o   Participant contributions and earnings on those contributions vest immediately.
  - o   Safe Harbor matching contributions and earnings on those contributions vest immediately.
  - o   Non Safe Harbor matching contributions vest under defined contribution rules.

One other note…Your employer can require that you work for the company for 1 year prior to participating in the plan. So, the number of years to vest can effectively be increased by one. Also, once you vest on your first funds, you are vested in all funds. In other words, if you have met vesting requirements, all future contributions vest immediately.

Allowed Discrimination
Under certain circumstances, an employer is allowed to discriminate in favor of highly compensated employees.

In the first case, employers can discriminate in favor of employees that earn more than the Social Security Payroll Tax Income Limit ($127,200 in 2017). This is called Social Security Integration. Congress considers the amount of payroll tax the employer pays towards an employee's Social Security retirement benefit the equivalent of a retirement plan contribution. In essence, since an employer provides a Social Security contribution based on 100% of wages for those who earn under the income limit, and the employer provides a Social Security contribution based on less than 100% of wages for those who earn more than $127,200, the employer has the option to contribute a higher percentage of salary to the employer-sponsored retirement plan, usually a defined contribution plan, for those who earn over the Social Security limit.

If you are comparing one job offer to another, and one employer's plan offers Social Security integration and the other does not, then where your salary falls compared to the Social Security Payroll Tax Income Limit could influence which job offer you want to take.

In the second case, employers can skew a greater percentage of the employer's retirement plan contributions towards those who are "older"...much like catch-up contributions for IRAs and 401(k)s. This is called "Age Weighted" Contributions and will most likely benefit the readers of this book.

Non-Qualified Plans

Unlike qualified plans, a non-qualified plan can discriminate in favor of highly compensated employees. These plans can still provide tax benefits to employers and employees if they are constructed correctly. In general, to maintain tax benefits, the employee must have substantial risk of loss of the contributed funds or some event must occur for the employee to gain access to the funds.

Deferred Compensation. Much like a 401(k) plan, under a non-qualified, deferred compensation plan, an employee defers a portion of his or her income instead of receiving it. Deferred compensation plans do not have the annual contribution limits that apply to 401(k)s. Also, unlike a 401(k) plan, which places the deferred compensation into a trust, compensation deferred under a non-qualified, deferred compensation plan becomes a general liability of the employer. If the employer were to go bankrupt, the employee covered under the deferred compensation plan would have the same rights as a bond holder or a bank who made a loan to the company. If this does occur, the employee may receive pennies on the dollar, or perhaps nothing. It is this risk of loss that allows taxes on the wages to be deferred[48].

---

48 The deferred compensation is subject to Social Security and Medicare taxes (FICA) as of the later of (1) the date on which the services are performed

Restricted Stock Plan. Under a restricted stock plan, shares of stock, normally in the company worked for, are granted to an employee for free or at a reduced price. There will be a restriction on the stock that limits sale of the stock until an amount of time and potentially amount of time as an employee have passed. The excess of fair market value of stock over what the employee paid is taxable as ordinary income when the restriction ends. This could cost you a lot in taxes without corresponding "cash" to pay the tax _unless_ (pay attention this is important) the employee decides to take an 83(b) election. Under section 83(b), an employee has the option to elect to be taxed on the current spread between the fair market value and the price paid for the restricted stock, even though there is a substantial risk of forfeiture. If the election is selected, no tax is due when the restriction is lifted, and no tax will be due until sale of the stock. Perhaps even more importantly, the income earned upon sale will be taxed as capital gains, not ordinary income. As of this writing, capital gains rates are less than ordinary income tax rates. The paperwork and timing requirements to take this election are not insignificant, and you should consult with an Enrolled Agent (EA) or CPA prior to entering into a restricted stock plan. Really...don't do this yourself...really.

Incentive Stock Options (ISO) Plans. An incentive stock option is a "right" granted by a corporation to an employee to purchase company stock, usually at a set price. No income is recognized by the employee when receiving the option or upon its exercise (when the stock is bought). Income, specifically capital gains, is

---

or (2) when the deferred compensation is no longer subject to a substantial risk of forfeiture. From a practical standpoint, most highly compensated employees will not owe Social Security when paid out because the employee most likely earned more than the upper limit for Social Security withholding. Medicare taxes would be due though, as there is no income limit for Medicare taxes (1.45%)

only recognized when the stock is sold[49]. As mentioned previously, capital gains are taxed at a lower rate than ordinary income. It is important to realize there are AMT ramifications to ISO plans. Specifically, when you exercise the option, the bargain element (the difference between the exercise price and the fair market value of the stock) is treated as income for calculating AMT[50]. If you will be subject to AMT, and many of you will be, you'll want to account for this when offered an ISO. Several requirements, such as maximum duration and limits to the time the option can be held, exist for the plan to qualify as an ISO plan, but these restrictions will be the responsibility of your employer.

Nonqualified Stock Option (NSO) Plans. An NSO, like an ISO, is a "right" granted to purchase stock at a set price, but the right is granted on a "discriminatory" basis. An option granted under an NSO plan does not have the duration and/or holding requirements of an ISO plan. Therefore, the options are taxed differently than those granted under an ISO. In most cases, there will not be a tax due when the NSOs are granted.[51] Assuming the NSOs were not taxed when granted, there will be tax due when the NSOs are exercised. Specifically, the bargain element (the difference between the purchase price and the fair market value) is taxed as wages. This means you will owe income, Social Security, and Medicare taxes on the bargain element. Think about that for a moment, you'll owe taxes on income you haven't received. All you have done is _spend_ money...purchasing stock at a discount.

---

49 The capital gain is calculated by subtracting the price paid when executing the option from the sale price of the stock. To be treated as capital gains the stock must be held until 2 years from the issue of the option or 1 year from the date of exercise of the option, whichever is later.

50 Think about that. You could have "income" but all you have done is buy stock.

51 This is the case because in most cases the NSOs have no "readily ascertainable fair market value" at the date of grant. If the NSO has a "readily ascertainable fair market value," the value is taxed as ordinary income.

When you sell the stock purchased via the NSO plan, you'll pay taxes on any capital gains (the basis of the stock will be the fair market value of the stock when you exercised the option).

Stock Appreciation Rights (SAR). Did you have an imaginary friend when you were a kid? If you did, then SARs will make sense to you. A SAR is an imaginary unit that is linked to the value of the company's common stock. A SAR usually is based on the fair market value of the stock and has an exercise date. In some cases, a SAR will have a different price based on a formula. A SAR gains value as the stock price goes up and goes down in value as the price of the stock goes down.[52] Income is recognized (becomes taxable) when the SAR is exercised. The amount of income is the amount resulting from the sale of the SAR (essentially the gain in the value of the stock).

Phantom Stock. No...you're not getting partial ownership of an F-4. Phantom stock is very similar to a SAR plan. Like a SAR, the phantom stock is not ownership of the company, but ties the executive's future compensation to the performance of the company's stock. Unlike a SAR plan, it does not have an exercise date, but it does have a timeframe and can pay out the entire value of the stock vice paying appreciation only in a SAR plan. When you receive compensation as a part of a phantom stock plan, you will be subject to income tax. You also will be subject to payroll taxes (FICA) when the services required by the plan are performed or you become vested in the plan.

There are other non-qualified plans, but as mentioned previously, they all share two very important characteristics. First, your income under the plan is not guaranteed, since there is a substantial risk of loss. This is why you don't pay taxes on some of the compensation until you get it. Second, the tax ramifications are not simple and you should get competent tax advice if you are offered

---

52 The value of a SAR will not be less than the value or formula price on the date of grant.

one of these employer sponsored plans. While you're at it, if you get offered one of these plans, have a drink. You've "made it."

Other Employee Benefits

Group Life Insurance. Your employer may provide group life insurance as a benefit of your employment...much like SGLI. Unlike SGLI, many employers provide this coverage at no cost to the employee. *Unlike in the military, benefits provided by an employer are taxable compensation unless exempted or excluded from income in the Tax Code.* In the case of life insurance, if the plan is structured properly, which is up to your employer, not you, the premiums for up to $50,000 of life insurance are tax exempt. If your employer provides you more than $50,000 in coverage, the premiums paid by your employer for the insurance coverage are taxable to you. You might still want to take the insurance as group policies generally do not have strict underwriting standards, and the tax you pay on the premium should be less than what the insurance would cost you on the commercial market.

Flexible Spending Arrangements (FSA). An FSA is offered through a cafeteria plan, in which an employee defers a portion of his or her income and directs the employer to contribute it into a dedicated account. The benefit of these accounts is that any funds used for qualified expenses are excluded from income. In most cases, these accounts are use or lose. If you don't spend the money in the plan year, the amount remaining will be forfeited. Some potential uses of an FSA for a retired Military Member include unreimbursed medical expenses[53] such as co-pays, and dependent

---

53 "Thanks" to ObamaCare, the annual limit for Medical FSA deferments has been reduced to $2,500. You can, however, carry forward up to $500 of unused Medical FSA deferments.

care[54]. I hope you noticed it is dependent care, not child care. So, if you end up caring for your parents, you may be able to take advantage of this benefit. One final note, in the case of medical expenses, if you spend money on medical expenses faster than you are putting money into the FSA, you'll get reimbursed for the expenses until you reach the amount you are planning to defer for the year. This is not the case for dependent care reimbursements. Dependent care expenses are reimbursed up to the current balance of the account.

Health Savings Accounts (HSA). An HSA can be used to pay for unreimbursed medical expenses. Unfortunately (actually it's probably "Fortunately"), as a military retiree and TRICARE beneficiary you will not qualify for an HSA because coverage under a high deductible health plan is an eligibility requirement. TRICARE is not a high deductible plan…yet.

What if I'm Lead?

Some of you, like me, will start your own business and you'll be "lead." You have some other things to worry about and some benefits employees don't have…

Be a Business. If you're going to be in business, be in business. The first step is to form a business. I have two recommendations for you. First, don't conduct business as a partnership or sole proprietor. The liability that transfers to your personal assets is more than you should accept. While the decision is more complicated than can be explained in a sentence or two, most likely you will want to form an LLC or an S Corporation[55]. Technically, the IRS doesn't

---

54 There is an IRS annual limit of $5,000 that can be contributed per family unit (you and your spouse), even if both taxpayers have access to an FSA.

55 Several "advisors" recommend starting an S Corporation and paying yourself a small salary and paying out the remainder as dividends to avoid self-employment taxes. Be very careful if you go this route. The salary must be reasonable and if you are providing personal services (i.e. consulting) it is,

recognize the LLC as a form of business so the LLC will be taxed as a sole proprietor, partnership, or corporation depending on what you chose. Second, if you are a business, you most likely need a business license, even if you are a consultant and in some locales such as Northern Virginia you'll get to pay business personal property taxes on your desk, chair and other business property.

You Have a Lot of Retirement Plan Options

As a business owner you will have a lot of options to use to save for your retirement. Here are some of them.

Traditional/Roth IRAs. As you start your business, you might want to use either a Traditional or a Roth IRA. Like any other American with earned income, you can contribute the lesser of $5,500 (plus $1,000 catch up for those age 50 or older) or your earned income to an IRA. Assuming you don't have another job that provides a retirement plan, you will be able to deduct the Traditional IRA contributions regardless of your income[56]. If your income is low (in the 15% tax bracket) as you start the business, you might want to consider contributing to a Roth IRA, which has the same contribution limits as a Traditional IRA. This is due to the fact that once you are fully retired, your income tax rate is likely to be higher than 15%. So you pay tax at 15% when you make the contribution, but you'll avoid 25% or higher tax rates when you take the money out. Good deal.

Individual 401(k). An Individual 401(k) is really not any different than a 401(k). There are some reduced record-keeping/reporting requirements as the 401(k) starts because the balance is low and you are the only participant. The unique opportunity

---

in my mind, difficult to support a position that reasonable compensation is considerably less than what the client pays you.

56 If you're covered by a retirement plan at work, then your income must be below certain limits to be able to deduct contributions to a Traditional IRA.

in an Individual 401(k) is that you can declare the first $18,000 ($24,000 if age 50 or older)[57] after accounting for self-employment taxes as "wages" and contribute the entire amount to the Individual 401(k). Additionally, you can contribute up to an additional 20%[58] of business net income/self-employment income into the 401(k) as a profit-sharing contribution. The maximum you can contribute including both the deferred wages and profit sharing contributions is $53,000[59]. The profit sharing contributions are "deducted" from the business's net income.

SEP (SEP-IRA). A Simplified Employee Pension Plan (SEP) essentially allows for _employer_ contributions to an individual's (employee or owner) IRA. The contributions are deductible to the employer. The accounts are owned and managed by the beneficiary, not the employer. Unlike a 401(k), all contributions to a SEP are calculated as a percentage (20% for the business owner) up to a total contribution of $53,000. Just to be clear though, to contribute $53,000, you would need to have net income in the amount of $265,000.

SIMPLE Plan. A Savings Incentive Match Plan for Employees (SIMPLE) Plan is similar to an individual 401(k) in that employees electively defer pre-tax income into an account on their behalf. SIMPLE plans have a lower limit on deferrals, and as of 2017 the limit is $12,500 with a $3,000 catch-up for those 50 or older. A SIMPLE plan requires mandatory matching funds from the business owner. Owners can deduct the matching contributions.

It is important to note that if a business owner plans to expand the business over time, in most cases future employees will need to be covered by the same retirement plan to maintain the retirement plan's favorable tax treatment. You'll want to consider this prior to starting the plan.

---

57 2017 Amounts

58 In some documents, you'll see 25%, but once you account for self-employment taxes, the actual amount you can contribute is 20% of net income.

59 2017 Amount

Taxes

Being self-employed brings some tax breaks, but it also brings some additional taxes.

Say Hello to My Little Friend, "Self-Employment Taxes." As I mentioned earlier, if you go into business you need to comprehend the impact of self-employment taxes. Actually, self-employment taxes are just Social Security and Medicare taxes. But, as a self-employed individual, you get the opportunity to pay both sides of the taxes. Instead of paying 7.65% of income in FICA, you'll pay 15.3% in self-employment taxes. Combine this with a likely 25% Federal Marginal Tax Rate and 5% or so in state income taxes, and you're looking at only keeping 55% of your self-employment income. One bit of good news is, like employment income, the Social Security portion of self-employment taxes (12.4%) is only due on the first $127,200 of combined self-employment income and wages.

You'll Get Some Good Tax Breaks. As a business owner, you are able to deduct expenses that are ordinary and necessary for the operation of your business. In other words, if you are spending a buck so that you can make a buck (let's hope it is more than one buck) you can deduct the expense. You are able to deduct many of the same expenses as an employee, but since you are self-employed you are not limited to deducting only those expenses that exceed 2% of your AGI. You also can deduct some medical insurance expenses, such as long-term care insurance, without having to meet the 10% AGI limit to deduct the expenses as an itemized deduction.

An Old "Urban Myth"

I've heard several times that if you start a business and don't have a profit in 3 out of 5 years, the activity does not qualify as a business and is therefore a hobby. This isn't exactly true. The IRS presumes an activity is business if it has shown a profit in 3 out of the last

5 years. Beyond that, the IRS looks at the individual situation to determine if your business is a business or a hobby. Some of the things the IRS looks at are:

- Does the time and effort put into the activity indicate an intention to make a profit?
- Does the taxpayer depend on income from the activity?
- If there are losses, are they due to circumstances beyond the taxpayer's control or did they occur in the start-up phase of the business?
- Has the taxpayer changed methods of operation to improve profitability?
- Does the taxpayer or his/her advisors have the knowledge needed to carry on the activity as a successful business?
- Has the taxpayer made a profit in similar activities in the past?
- Does the activity make a profit in some years?
- Can the taxpayer expect to make a profit in the future from the appreciation of assets used in the activity?

Obviously, you can't sustain losses for a long time, perhaps with the exception of rental real estate, and still be in business. But, there isn't a hard and fast rule.

CHAPTER 5

CHECK-6

There a more than a couple of "threats" you didn't have or could ignore while you were on active duty. They lay in wait for you so you need to watch out for them and plan for them. Start by paying attention to your taxes.

Uncle Is Waiting

Let me see if I can make you mad...your taxes are low. Actually your taxes are very low and your Uncle Sam is waiting for you to pick up your share. Let me give you an example. If your Basic Allowance of Housing (BAH), Basic Allowance for Subsistence (BAS) and uniform allowance, if applicable, were deemed wages/taxable income, your total tax bill would go up by between $6,000 and 7,500 annually, depending on where you live and your rank. And here is the kicker, an E-9 will pay more than an O-6. That has to do with Social Security taxes. Many of you who are colonels or captains (O-6s) have noticed that your pay is higher in December (hint: It isn't a Christmas bonus). This is because O-6s can earn in excess of $127,200, so the additional income subject to taxation would not be subject to Social Security taxation. E-9s would remain below the threshold and pay Social Security on the entire amount of BAH, BAS and Uniform Allowance. But that is now. What will happen after you retire? Let's look at one example.

Bull is a retired Colonel and he has a pretty good job on the outside. His total income between retirement and his new job is $160,000. This also equals his AGI. Bull used his GI Bill for Junior, but his two daughters are still in college, and he is paying their expenses. Bull has limited deductions, and he is in the 28% marginal tax bracket. Bull's boss comes in one day and offers him a promotion with a salary increase of $20,000 per year. Bull starts thinking about how he will spend all that extra income. But before he does, why don't we take a look at the tax impact of the raise? Here is how Bull's taxes will change/increase:

What We Know about Bull's Income:

Income	$160,000
Potential raise	$20,000
Marginal tax rate	28%

Tax Calculation on Raise:

Income tax	$20,000 x 0.28 =	$5,600
Loss of the American Opportunity Credit*		$5,000
Medicare tax (1.45%)	$20,000 x 0.0145 =	$ 290
Social security tax (6.2%)	$20,000 x 0.062 =	$1,240
State income tax (assumes Virginia, 5.75%)	$20,000 x 0.0575 =	$1,150
TOTAL TAX ON $20,000 RAISE		**$13,280**

*Bull's income is now too high to take this credit.

Old Bull won't have quite as much money to spend as he thought he would; he'll see only about 34% (or $6,720) of his $20,000 raise. And guess what? This is about to become your reality too. You may not believe it, but you are about to become one of the "rich." Welcome. Depending on who you talk to, if you're making $133,000 per year (per household), then you are in the top 10% of Americans in terms of income (not necessarily wealth). And Uncle wants you to pay. Here are just some of the ways he will be coming after you...

- As shown in the example above, if your AGI exceeds $180,000 per year, you lose the ability to claim the American Opportunity Credit.

- Once your income reaches $118,000 single ($186,000 married), you begin to lose the ability to contribute to a Roth IRA.
- At $200,000 of income single ($250,000 married), you become subject to certain ObamaCare Surtaxes.
- At $261,500 single ($313,800 married), you start to lose itemized deductions and exemptions.[60]

Don't Do a W-4

Actually, you won't have a choice. Your new employer will make you complete a W-4. But, based on what I've seen, I think most of you go through the "exercise" like this. The HR person hands you a W-4 as part of your in-processing. You think to yourself, "I'm an operator. I convinced my new boss I can make things happen. I need to get to work and prove how valuable I am. Why am I wasting time on paperwork? Oh hell…Married with 4 worked fine on active duty, it should work fine here." It won't. The way withholding works will set you up for a big surprise come next April. Here is why. Your employer may know you are a retired military member and you receive a pension. But, the amount of the pension won't be used to calculate your withholding. Your employer will withhold taxes based on the assumption that the first dollar you earn there is your first dollar earned. As shown in Figure 1, in reality the first dollar you earn at your new job is your 50,000th (E-9) or 70,000th (O-6) dollar earned.

---

60 Dollar limits are 2017 numbers.

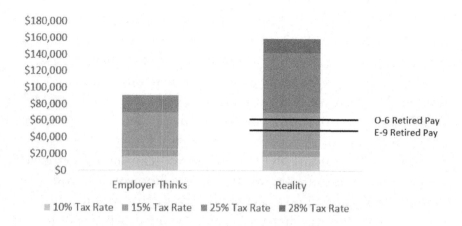

Figure 1: Include your military retirement pay when filling out your W-4 to avoid unwelcome surprises.[61]

As the chart shows, your employer is paying you $90,000 per year and withholds taxes based upon that amount of income[62]. Your employer will withhold some taxes at 10%, some at 15%, and a little at 25%. But in reality, if you are a retired O-6 with around $70,000 of retirement income, your employer should withhold from most of your income, starting at the first dollar, at 25% and a bit of your income at 28%. If you retire as an E-9, then a portion of your employment income should be withheld at 15% but the remainder will need to be withheld at 25% or 28%.

Now, I know none of you would complete your W-4 the way I described. But, I am surprised at how many retired senior leaders, mostly colonels and captains, I meet who owe between $7,000 and $8,000 in taxes their first full year in retirement. So, what to do about it?

---

61 Excludes any deductions.

62 For the purposes of this discussion I will ignore deductions and exemptions

The best thing for you to do to avoid surprises is to complete an IRS Form 1040-ES. Once you receive your first RAS[63] and pay-stub from your employer, you can complete the form. In essence, what you'll do is complete your tax return with estimated numbers. If the result shows you will owe taxes, you can go to MyPay and increase withholding on your retired pay. The IRS doesn't care where the withheld taxes come from, just that you withhold enough. I recommend MyPay because you can set a specific additional dollar amount to be withheld. In other words, if your calculations show you will owe $3,000 and there are six months left in the year, you can instruct DFAS, via MyPay, to withhold an additional $500 per month from your retired pay.

If you're not going to go through the effort of completing a Form 1040-ES, at least spend some time on completing your W-4. Be sure to go through the total calculation on page 2 of Form W-4.

If you're unwilling or unable to do either of the above, then in your first full year of retirement make sure you withhold between $2,000 and $2,500 in Federal income tax per month. This assumes your income will be in the vicinity of $150,000 and you don't have extremely large itemized deductions. To put it another way, your taxes for a year other than the year you retire will be between $20,000 and $30,000 per year. While that seems like a lot, if you can get your taxable income[64] down to around $120,000 and pay the average tax rate for that amount of income of around 18%, your tax bill will be $21,600. If your income is higher or your deductions are lower, you can expect to pay more.

Watch Out For ObamaCare Surtaxes

Two of the many tax increases included in ObamaCare are called Medicare Surtaxes. You may need to watch out for both of them.

---

63 Retiree Account Statement – This replaces your LES.
64 AGI minus deductions and exemptions.

The first ObamaCare surtax applies to earned income/wages[65]. If your earned income exceeds $250,000 married filing jointly or $200,000 filing single, you will be subject to this tax. The tax is 0.9% of your earned income that exceeds the limit. Interestingly, your employer will start withholding this tax if your wages exceed $200,000 no matter what your filing status, single or married. Conversely, if you and your spouse earn $199,999 each, the tax will not be withheld from either salary. The result is you will owe $1,350 in additional Medicare tax when you file your income tax return.

The second ObamaCare surtax concerns net investment income, which includes[66]:

- Interest.
- Dividends.
- Annuities.
- Royalties.
- Rents.
- Net gain attributable to the disposition of property other than property held in a trade or business. It does include 1250 gains from the sale of rental property.

The tax is called the Net Investment Income Tax (NIIT), and it is 3.8%, which is applied to your net investment income. Similar to the surtax on wages, this tax applies to income above certain thresholds. Unlike for the wage surtax, your military retirement _will_ be included in the calculation of this threshold. The dollar amount of the threshold is the same as for the surtax on wages, $250,000 for those married filing jointly and $200,000 for those

---

65 As a reminder, military retirement income and Social Security income as well are _not_ included as "earned" income.

66 It is important to note that distributions from qualified retirement plans or arrangements (IRAs) are _not_ considered net investment income.

filing single[67]. In this case, the surtax is only applicable if total income exceeds the threshold and a portion of the income is net investment income. You do get to deduct the portion of your state income tax that you pay as result of this income from the net investment income when figuring out the tax owed. Similar to the W-4 discussion, a chart might help out; see Figure 2.

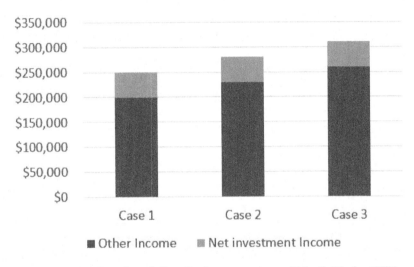

Figure 2: In Case 2 and Case 3, the taxpayer would be liable for NIIT.

In Case 1 there is $200,000 of other income and $50,000 in net investment income. Assuming the taxpayer is married filing jointly, no NIIT would be due. In the second case, there is $230,000 of other income and still $50,000 of net investment income. The tax will be due on $30,000 (the portion of the net investment income above the threshold). The NIIT will be $1,140 and will be added to any other taxes on the income. In Case 3, there is $260,000 in other income and the net investment income remains at $50,000.

_____

67 Married filing jointly is often abbreviated as MFJ. I once saw single abbreviated as SAH for Single and Happy…just checking to see if you're reading the footnotes.

The NIIT will be due on the entire $50,000 (in this case it would be due on the $50,000 regardless of if the taxpayer is filing married filing jointly or single) and would amount to $1,900.

If you land a job that puts you close to the threshold, you might want to keep an eye on this. Even if you don't land the Beltway Bandit job, you could still end up owing the tax if you are not careful. There are two specific cases I watch for. First, Roth Conversions. As mentioned, distributions from an IRA are not subject to the NIIT. But a conversion to a Roth does produce income, and that income could put a portion of your net investment income above your threshold. The second case is the result of selling that good old rental property. If you've held the property for a while and accumulated significant depreciation, you could become subject to the tax. When you sell the property the depreciation will, in most cases, be subject to taxation. Specifically the amount you sell the house for that exceeds your adjusted basis up to the original basis is called 1250 gains. These gains are subject to taxation at a maximum rate of 25%. But for the purposes of this discussion, the 1250 gains also increase your income _and_ your net investment income and could subject you to the NIIT. This income will be counted even if you can qualify the property as your primary residence under the 2 out of 5 year rule[68].

Be Very Careful with IRAs

One of the most complex and confusing area of tax law is the rules that cover IRAs. It starts with the acronym IRA. Now, I love a good acronym as much as the next guy, but you have to _know_ what the acronym actually means. Most of us assume IRA stands

---

68 If you lived in the house for 2 out of the previous 5 years (potentially longer if you moved out of the house due to PCS orders), you can exclude the gain that exceeds your original basis plus improvements up to a limit of $500,000 if filing MFJ or $250,000 if filing single.

for Individual Retirement Account. In reality, IRA stands for Individual Retirement Arrangement. Why am I splitting hairs on this one? Because you can only have one Individual Retirement Arrangement even though it might be composed of several accounts (perhaps at different mutual fund companies or different accounts at the same mutual fund company).

There is a rule that says you can do one rollover per IRA per year without tax consequences. If you do a second, the rollover is deemed a taxable distribution. To clarify, a rollover is when you take possession of the funds and re-deposit them into an IRA within 60 days. When you transfer funds/assets directly from one IRA custodian to another without taking possession of the funds/assets, it is not considered a rollover. Back to our acronym. If you assume that IRA stands for Individual Retirement Account, you could easily make the mistake of making rollovers from two different accounts and get a surprise tax bill when the IRS determines the second rollover was a non-qualified distribution subject to taxes and, if you're younger than 59 ½, penalties.

Speaking of rollovers, you can never do a rollover from an inherited IRA[69]. If you try to do a rollover, you most likely won't be able to re-deposit it. Even if you can, it won't qualify and you'll be subject to tax, but no penalty, as you can take money out of an inherited IRA as fast as you want and as soon as you want without penalty.

Please Allow Me to Introduce Myself...

Besides having the opportunity to pay a higher tax rate, you may get the opportunity to pay the Alternative Minimum Tax (AMT). The AMT or versions of the AMT have been around since 1969,

---

69 The one exception is if you are the spouse of the deceased IRA owner. Then you could claim the inherited IRA as your own and do a rollover after that.

and the current AMT became law in 1982. The purpose of the AMT is to make sure that the "rich" pay their fair share of taxes. As mentioned before, the definition of rich is somewhat fungible. I see a lot of retired Military members who get hit with AMT. So, just how does the AMT work?

The AMT is pretty darn close to a flat tax. There are two rates...26% and 28%[70]. To calculate AMT, take your taxable income after reducing it for itemized deductions and make adjustments to that income based on what you had for deductions and special types of income. You then reduce the income by a standard exemption[71]. This is considered your AMT income. This income is then multiplied by the appropriate tax rate. If the result of this calculation is higher than your tax as calculated under the normal tax rules, you increase your total tax bill to reach the amount calculated under the AMT regimen.

Making more money is not the only thing that can make you subject to AMT, and, in fact, once you get into the 33% or higher bracket, your exposure to AMT goes down. What makes you subject to the AMT? There are a lot of things that can increase your opportunity to pay the AMT, but I see four main culprits commonly amongst retired Military members.

- **Higher Income.** Incomes in the range of $150,000 to $275,000 have a higher probability of being subject to AMT. This is especially true if combined with one or more of the other factors that can trigger the AMT.
- **Larger Families.** You might have noticed when I described the calculation of AMT that you start with your income after

---

70 The 26% bracket ends at $186,300 of AMT Income.

71 In 2017 the exemption amount for taxpayers who are married filing jointly is $84,500 and $54,300 for those filing single. The exemption begins to phase out when AMT income exceeds $159,700 married filing jointly and $119,700 for those filing single.

itemized deductions. This means you start with income _before_ exemptions. In other words you "loose" your exemptions, and the more your exemptions reduce your normal taxes, the more likely you will be subject to AMT.

- **Lots of State Income Tax.** There are certain itemized deductions you must add back on to your AMT starting income when you calculate AMT. State income tax paid is one of them. If you live in a state with a high state income tax rate or you have a lot of income subject to state income tax, look out for the AMT.

- **Miscellaneous Itemized Deductions.** All those job hunting expenses you took as an itemized deduction get added back to your income when calculating AMT. So do the rest of your miscellaneous itemized deductions. I'd still deduct them if you can[72], but be ready to give them back when calculating AMT.

There are a few other notes, warnings and cautions when it comes to AMT, and if you suspect you might be subject to AMT, then you should make sure you understand the other things that can subject you to the AMT before you make financial decisions. As an example, you might decide to invest in tax-free municipal bonds due to your otherwise high marginal tax rate. But, if those municipal bonds are considered "private-activity bonds," like funding for a football stadium, the interest on the bonds must be included in your income when calculating AMT.

There isn't much you can do to avoid the AMT, or at least many of the options aren't very feasible. I don't really see you getting rid of a child to avoid the AMT. The best you can do is be aware of it and make sure you don't do anything avoidable that would increase your AMT.

---

72 Miscellaneous itemized deductions are subject to a floor of 2% of AGI.

Got Any More Good News?

The reality is that once you recognize income[73], there are essentially four ways to reduce your taxes. They are:

1. Spend a dollar to save a quarter (assuming a 25% marginal tax rate).
2. Spend a dollar to save a dollar.
3. Invest/defer a dollar to save a quarter.
4. Account for a dollar to save a quarter.

Spend a Dollar to Save a Quarter. When you deduct your mortgage interest or property taxes or any other deduction, you are in fact, spending a dollar to save a quarter. You won't get rich this way, but the Federal Government is helping you afford your house or subsidizing your state income tax bill.

Spend a Dollar to Save a Dollar. Some credits will reimburse you dollar for dollar if you spend money on the targeted expense. A perfect example of this is the American Opportunity Credit (AOC). If you qualify for the AOC, the government will reduce your taxes dollar for dollar on the first $2,000 paid for qualified education expenses. The AOC also illustrates not all credits are dollar for dollar; it reduces your taxes 25 cents for each dollar between $2,000 and $4,000 spent on qualified education expenses.

Invest/Defer a Dollar to Save a Quarter. Now we're starting to get to the good stuff. If you invest in your 401(k)/403(b)/TSP or Traditional IRA[74], you will reduce your current tax bill by 25% of the amount contributed, assuming a 25% marginal tax rate. Another option is to defer recognition of a gain on a rental prop-

---

73 Recognized income is a tax term that signifies when income becomes taxable. For example, when your mutual fund pays out dividends, you recognize income even though most likely the value of your account stays the same.

74 Traditional IRA contributions will not be deductible for all taxpayers. If you are covered by a retirement plan at work, then your income must be below certain thresholds to qualify for the deduction.

erty through a 1031 exchange. If you do, for each dollar in income you defer, you'll save 25 cents in taxes. It is important to note you could eventually pay taxes on the deferred income when you take the money out of your retirement account or sell the exchanged property.

Account for a Dollar to Save a Quarter. When you depreciate a rental property or other business asset, you account for a dollar of loss, and it offsets a dollar of income and reduces your taxes by 25 cents. Like the previous topic, you might owe taxes on the depreciation you took when you sell the asset.

AGI

There is one other important thing to know. The single most important number on your tax return is your AGI. Your AGI controls many deductions, credits, and reductions in deductions and exemptions. Some examples include[75] (you've seen some of these before):

- The ability to deduct losses from actively managed real estate phases out between $100,000 and $150,000 of AGI.
- The ability to exclude US Savings Bond Interest used to pay qualified education expenses phases out between $117,250 and $147,250 (MFJ) and between $78,180 and $93,150 (single).
- Eligibility for the American Opportunity Credit phases out between $160,000 and $180,000 (MFJ) and between $80,000 and $90,000 (single).
- Medical deductions are limited to only the amount that exceeds 10% of AGI, and miscellaneous itemized deductions are only deductible to the extent they exceed 2% of AGI.
- Exemptions and a certain portion of itemized deductions are reduced if AGI exceeds $261,500/$313,800 (Single/MFJ).

---

75 Dollar amounts are for 2017.

What can you do to control your AGI? A lot, but not all, of the things you can do fall in the category of invest/defer a dollar to save a quarter.

Contribute to Your Employer Offered Retirement Plan. If your employer offers a 401(k), 403(b) or TSP, the single best thing you can do to reduce your current taxes is to contribute the maximum amount to the account. I'm not talking about the amount to get the maximum employer match, but rather the maximum amount allowed by law. As of this writing, the maximum amount allowed is $18,000 and if you are 50 or older[76] you can contribute an additional $6,000 for a total of $24,000. This can reduce your taxes by a whole lot more than your marginal tax rate. Let's go back to our example above with two kids in college and look at it in reverse. If the retired senior leader has an AGI of $180,000 and contributes $20,000 to a 401(k), that will reduce his or her taxes by $11,750[77] or a 59% return on investment.

Contribute to a Traditional IRA (or Self-Employed Retirement Plan). If you don't have a retirement plan at work you can contribute to a Traditional IRA _and_ deduct the contributions, regardless of your income[78]. Unfortunately, the contribution limits to a Traditional IRA and most self-employed retirement plans are lower than those allowed to a 401(k) plan or its cousins. The limits for a Traditional IRA is $5,500, with an additional $1,000 catch-up contribution allowed for those 50 or older[79].

Revenue Ruling 78-161/Strickland Decision. This is a one-time good deal and applies to those who are rated less than 50%

---

76 The catch up contributions go into effect in the year you turn 50.

77 The amount saved is less than the amount of tax increase in the prior example because Social Security and Medicare taxes are still payable on the $20,000.

78 Income becomes an issue for deductibility if you are covered by a retirement plan at work. If your income exceeds the limit, you can still contribute to a Traditional IRA, but the contributions are not deductible.

79 2017 amounts

disabled by the VA. The reason it applies to your taxes is because it will take some time for the VA to determine your disability rating. For some of you, it will take more than some time. A lot more. During that time you will be accruing benefits. If you end up being rated less than 50% disabled, that means your RAS[80] will be incorrect and your 1099-R[81] will be too. Or more specifically, the government will report more taxable income than it actually should. They won't correct the discrepancy either, and if you don't exercise your rights under this ruling, you will pay more income tax than you should.

Believe it or not, this goes back to the Vietnam era. A retired Army member, Strickland, sued the government based on the fact that a portion of his retirement pay should have been tax-free since the disability rating was retroactive to 1 month after his retirement. The court agreed. In the decision, the 4th Circuit stated the taxpayer was entitled to exclude from gross income part of the payments previously received as retirement pay. The IRS agreed with the 4th Circuit (they don't always agree with the court...believe it or not) and Revenue Ruling 78-161 documents that agreement.

This means if you end up being rated less than 50% disabled, you can make an adjustment to income to reflect the amount of retroactive VA benefits you should have received and the corresponding reduction in taxable income. If the time the VA takes to resolve your claim spans more than one tax year, you can amend a previous year's tax return by filing a Form 1040-X.

You can't wait forever though to file your amended return. Under "normal" circumstances, you can amend a tax return for up to 3 years after you file it. Congress did realize the VA doesn't always act quickly, and there is a specific exception to the statute

---

80 Retiree Account Statement – This replaces your LES. Come on, you have to learn the new terms!

81 Your taxable retirement income will be reported to the IRS on a Form 1099-R instead of a W-2.

of limitations rules for normal amended returns. The exception is codified in IRC Section 6511(d)(8), and while I don't normally like to quote the law, I'm going to do it here. It's that complicated...

Special Rules when uniformed services retired pay is reduced as a result of award of disability compensation
(A) Period of Limitation on filing claim

If the claim for credit or refund relates to an overpayment of tax imposed by subtitle A on account of
(i) the reduction of uniformed services retired pay computed under section 1406 or 1407 of Title 10 United States Code or
(ii) the waiver of such pay under section 5304 of Title 38 of such Code as a result of an award of compensation under Title 38 of such Code pursuant to a determination by Secretary of Veterans Affairs, the 3-year period of limitation prescribed in subsection (a) shall be extended, for purposes of permitting a credit or refund based upon the amount of such reduction of waiver, until the end of the 1-year period beginning on the date of such determination.

(B) Subparagraph (A) shall not apply with respect to any taxable year which began more than 5 years before the date of such determination

Now that I've quoted the law, and I do apologize for that, let me try to explain it. First, you have 1 year from the date of the VA determination to file any amended returns[82]. Second, how many years can you go back? You start with the date of letter of determination. Then you count back 5 years and you can amend a

---

82 While it isn't clearly stated, I don't think Congress intended to limit your ability to file an amended return to less than the 3 years all taxpayers have under "normal" circumstances.

return for any tax year that began on or after that date. I suspect most of you will not receive a determination letter dated 1 Jan, since it is a holiday, so from a practical standpoint you'll be able to file an amended return for the 4 years prior to the date of the determination.

The IRS and the Courts aren't particularly flexible on this issue. In *Haas v the United States* the case went as follows:

- Haas retired in 2001.
- The VA rating decision was issued on 1 Dec 2009.
- Haas files for refunds for 2001–2008.
- Plaintiff's statute of limitation for filing his refund claim was extended for 1 year from that date, or until 1 Dec 2010.
- The 5-year maximum limits the extended statute of limitation to the 5 tax years preceding the date of determination.
- Five years before the date of determination is 1 Dec 2004.
- Because the 2004 tax-year began on 1 Jan 2004, the 2005 tax year is the earliest year for which Haas may receive the benefit of the extended statute of limitations.
- The Court determined Haas's refund claims for 2001–2004 are not subject to that extension.

And, just in case you're wondering, based on other anecdotal evidence, the IRS has little to no patience for returns filed after the 1-year extension.

But wait! There's more! If you think you might find yourself in this situation, you might want to consider filing a protective claim. When you file a protective claim for refund, you are essentially informing the IRS that due to a government proceeding, such as the VA process or a court case, you expect your tax situation to change retroactively and to do so beyond the statute of limitations. A protective claim for refund satisfies the statutory requirement to file a claim prior to the expiration of the statute of limitations. A protective claim must:

1. Have a written component.
2. Identify and describe the contingencies affecting the claim.
3. Be sufficiently clear and definite to alert the IRS as to the essential nature of the claim.
4. Identify a specific year or years for which a refund is sought.

Tax educators that I listen to recommend you use a Form 1040-X to file a protective claim. It doesn't appear a 1040-X is required, but it might be a good idea.

There is one final area of consideration when it comes to IRR 78-161, and it applies to Combat Related Special Compensation (CRSC). For most, if you are rated 50% or more disabled you will receive Concurrent Retirement and Disability Pay (CRDP). I think of it this way. Even if you are 50% or more disabled, your retired pay is reduced just like for those less than 50% disabled. The difference is for those 50% or more disabled, the VA offset gets filled back up with CRDP, which is taxable[83].

This isn't true for CRSC. CRSC is tax exempt, just like your VA compensation. To qualify for CRSC, you must have a disability that is combat or combat training related. To receive CRSC, you must proactively apply with your parent service for the compensation. If you receive a favorable determination, then the same principles that apply to the Strickland Decision may apply to you. It is important to note you can't receive CRSC and CRDP simultaneously, and CRSC is paid only on the disability that is combat or combat training related. Even with the tax benefit, accepting CRSC might not be your best choice.

Don't Give Your Cash to Charity. I didn't say don't support charitable causes, just don't give them cash. Instead, give them appreciated assets. If you've held an asset for more than 1 year, you can deduct the fair market value of the asset on the date of

---

83 This isn't technically how it works, but it is the best way to explain it. You won't see CRDP on your RAS...you do remember what an RAS is, don't you?

the gift[84]. By gifting appreciated assets, you get a tax deduction now, and you never recognize the gain you have accumulated on the asset. In fact, you can use the cash you would have given to the charity and immediately replace the gifted asset in your portfolio at a higher basis and keep your investment plan in place.

Think About Tax Efficient Investing. I listen to a fair bit of talk radio, maybe more than I should. It might not be healthy. But one thing I hear each and every day is that I need to "put gold in my IRA." That always causes me to pause and think. Is putting my gold in an IRA a good tax move? Assuming one is talking about a Traditional IRA (they don't say "Roth") and that I don't actively trade the gold, I don't think so. That is because an IRA shields current income from taxation, and a bar of gold doesn't produce any current income. Let's look at another example.

Imagine that 20 or so years ago, you and I had decided to purchase Apple stock. I decided to put mine into a Traditional IRA, and you decided to put yours into a taxable brokerage account. Over the years, Apple didn't pay many dividends, so you had minimal taxable income from the stock and I didn't defer taxes on much income. It came time to spend our money. I cashed out my IRA, and you sold your Apple stock. What are the tax consequences? I paid taxes at my marginal rate, 25% or 28% (or potentially higher). You paid 15% on the long-term capital gains (potentially higher if your income is significantly higher, but it will always be lower than your marginal rate). I paid almost twice the tax bill that you paid, just based on where the assets were located.

To prevent this type of scenario, there are some general rules on where to place your assets to invest them tax efficiently. Assuming you have access to the three main types of accounts, you should:

---

84 Under the general rule, gifts of capital gains property are limited to 30% of AGI. The gifts must be made to charities that most of us would recognize as such.

- Place assets that produce a lot of current income into tax-deferred accounts (401(k), TSP, Traditional IRA). This could include bonds and bond funds, real estate investment trusts, commodities funds.
- Place assets that produce little to no current income (or the income that is produced is in the form of qualified dividends) into taxable accounts. This could include large-cap stocks or funds, and developed markets stocks or funds.
- Put what you think will be your home runs into a Roth Account. Examples could be small-cap stocks or funds, or emerging markets funds.

Don't Fall for this Trap

Many of you will get a larger than planned refund in the year you retire. You might be tempted to think you've got everything wired and I was just trying to scare you earlier. Don't. A likely source of the refund is your Social Security withholding. As mentioned earlier, you only pay the Social Security portion of FICA on your first $127,200 of earned income/wages. When you work for one, and only one, employer for the entire year, your Social Security withholding will be correct. However, if you have more than one employer during a year and your total wages exceed $127,200, your employers will withhold too much Social Security tax. The good news is you'll get the withheld dollars back when you file your income tax return. The amount could be significant, because it will be 6.2% of the amount that exceeds the threshold. That amount will be added to your refund or will reduce the amount of taxes you owe. If you don't pay attention to the source of the refund, you could assume you have your withholding correct. Take the time to look at the source of your refund before you make decisions about the next year's withholding.

CHAPTER 6

WRAPPING IT UP

So there you have it. But before I wrap things up, I have some good news for you. The day you hang up your flight suit, ABUs or Class As, you're a millionaire. Regardless of whether you're a Senior NCO or Senior Officer, the actuarial value of your retirement income is in excess of $1,000,000. For many of you, the value exceeds $2,000,000. In other words, you would have to have $1,000,000–$3,000,000 invested to produce the income stream you will receive for the rest of your life.

On the other hand, as you saw in this book, your financial life will get more complicated and the stakes will be higher.

Before I started my business, I thought I could read a book and figure out just about anything. Two events caused me to change my opinion. The first was when I tried to put in crown molding in our master bedroom. After much swearing, re-dos and wasted time and resources, I have crown molding. It looks okay. It would look better if a professional had done it. The second event was when I tried to register my business as an Investment Advisory Firm. I started down the path of doing it myself…it was only paperwork. After a couple of months of frustration I hired a law firm to handle my registration and compliance requirements. Best decision I ever made. I pay them, but I can spend my time on issues that are a better use of my time.

Should you just read this book and figure it out? That's up to you. If you have the interest, inclination, and time to manage all your financial affairs I don't doubt that you can figure it out. You'll come up with an acceptable solution. On the other hand, if you want to spend your time on your highest value, best activities, you might want to consider hiring someone to manage your financial affairs. If you make this decision you should consider a few things.

Standard of Care. Not all "Financial Advisors" are required to treat you the same way. Individual advisor representatives who work for registered investment advisor firms are held to a fiduciary standard. This means that individual must always act your best interest. These individuals and firms are regulated by either the Securities and Exchange Commission or the individual state, depending on the size of the firm. On the other hand, registered representatives employed by broker dealers and insurance agents are held to a fair dealing standard, also known as the suitability standard. The suitability standard requires the advisor to make recommendations that are suitable, which generally means matches your risk tolerance. If an advisor can make more money with one recommendation versus another, and the extra money reduces your rate of return, the recommendation is okay under the suitability rule but not under the fiduciary standard. In most cases, I believe it is better to get advice that is in your best interest. It does get a little more complicated though.

Under recent DoL rules, all advisors must act in your best interest when advising on retirement accounts. Only registered investment advisors are required to meet a fiduciary standard on all accounts.

Also, some advisors are dual registered, so at certain times they are required to act in your best interest, and some other times they aren't. The best thing to do is simply ask, "Are you, by law, required to act in my best interest at all times?"

Competency. It is not all that hard to get the licenses required to give investment advice or to advise on insurance products. There is no guarantee your financial advisor has any specific educational background. In fact, the term *financial advisor* has no specific meaning in the law. One way to determine if the advisor you're talking to has the competency to give you advice about your financial life is to check for credentials. Some credentials aren't worth the ink it takes to print them. Some are pretty good. Here are some I'm aware of that have some teeth[85].

- **CERTIFIED FINANCIAL PLANNER™ (CFP®).** The CFP® designation is granted by the Certified Financial Planner Board of Standards. According to the CFP Board, "Although many professionals may call themselves 'financial planners,' CFP® professionals have completed extensive training and experience requirements and are held to rigorous ethical standards. They understand all the complexities of the changing financial climate and will make recommendations in your best interest."[86]
- **Enrolled Agent (EA).** EAs are licensed by the IRS. Per the IRS, "Enrolled agents are subject to a suitability check and must pass a three-part Special Enrollment Examination, which is a comprehensive exam that requires them to demonstrate proficiency in federal tax planning, individual and business tax return preparation, and representation. They must complete 72 hours of continuing education every 3 years."[87]
- **Chartered Financial Analyst (CFA).** The CFA designation is granted by the CFA Institute. The Institute states, "No credential is as widely regarded in the global financial industry for its rigorous focus on current investment knowledge,

85 As a matter of bias/disclosure, I hold the following credentials: CFP®, EA, AIF® (Accredited Investment Fiduciary). I also hold an MBA with an emphasis on Individual Financial Planning.

86 http://cfp.net/about-cfp-board/cfp-certification-the-standard-of-excellence

87 https://www.irs.gov/tax-professionals/understanding-tax-return-preparer-credentials-and-qualifications

analytical skill, and ethical standards as the Chartered Financial Analyst designation."[88]

- **Chartered Financial Consultant® (ChFC®).** The American College of Financial Services grants the ChFC® designation. Per their website, "Your Chartered Financial Consultant® has completed the most extensive educational program required for any financial services credential. Each ChFC® has taken nine or more college-level courses on all aspects of financial planning from The American College of Financial Services, a non-profit educator with the highest level of academic accreditation."[89]

- **Charter Life Insurance Underwriter.** According to Investopedia, "A chartered life underwriter (CLU) is a professional designation for individuals who wish to specialize in life insurance and estate planning. Individuals must complete five core courses and three elective courses, and successfully pass all eight 2-hour, 100-question examinations in order to receive the designation."[90]

If you are checking out a financial advisor who has other tri-graphs after his or her name, you should check out the credentials to see if they indicate much of anything. To do this, Google the designation and go to the web page. Don't spend any time on the consumer information. Look around the page and go to the "Become a Certified/Chartered Really Smart Guy" page. See what the requirements are. If the requirements are to take a weekend class and pay a fee, the certification might not be worth much. If on the other hand, it appears there are some real course work requirements and continuing education requirements, then it probably is worth considering when you make your decision.

---

88 https://www.cfainstitute.org/learning/investor/adviser/Pages/index.aspx

89 http://www.chfchigheststandard.com/

90 http://www.investopedia.com/terms/c/clu.asp

I'm biased, but I firmly believe in the CFP® designation and I recommend you use a CFP®. I also believe, based on your new life, you will want to consult with someone who is well versed in tax law. So, in my mind the CFP®–EA combination is pretty good. Not that there is anything wrong with the other designations above, but some of them are so specialized that the old saw, "If all you have is a hammer, then everything begins to look like a nail" begins to apply. If your educational background is almost entirely insurance based, then your solutions will likely involve insurance. A generalist, such as a CFP®, with a specialization that applies to your situation may be best.

Where can you find an advisor who will match your need? First of all, talk to your other trusted advisors such as a tax advisor or attorney. You might also talk to colleagues. If neither of these is an option, then you might want to check out the National Association of Personal Financial Advisors (NAPFA) at http://www.napfa.org/ or the Financial Planning Association at http://www.plannersearch.org/. Both sites have a "Find a Planner" function.

Well, that's it. Best of luck as you make your transition to the civilian world. I hope you find yourself in the place I am now–very proud of my military career and very happy where I am. God Speed.

APPENDIX A: SBP DECISION TREE FOR SPOUSE WITH PENSION

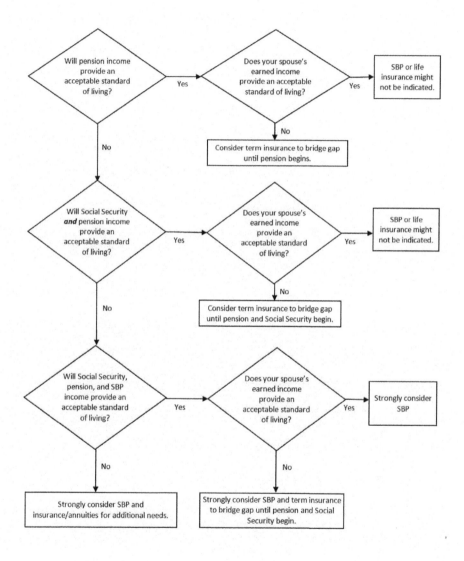

APPENDIX B: LET'S LOOK AT SOME SBP NUMBERS

As I mentioned in the first chapter, I couch the SBP in terms of transferring to the government inflation, longevity and, to a certain extent, return-sequence risk. In essence, you accept a lower pension, and in return, the government accepts the above-mentioned risks on your behalf. But if you don't take SBP, what is the risk to your spouse? I'll get to that in a moment. Before I do though, I want to review the risks I previously mentioned.

Inflation Risk. Inflation risk is the risk that your investment return is not sufficient to offset the effects of inflation. It could also apply in the case of insurance where the inflation rate is higher than you plan and your life insurance proceeds will not provide adequate capital to produce the buying power your spouse needs.

Longevity Risk. Longevity risk is that your money will run out before you check out from this world. As life expectancies increase, longevity risk is only increasing.

Return Sequence Risk. When we think about future returns, we often think/calculate that our returns will march along, giving us the average expected return each and every year. Real life doesn't work like that, and the worst thing that can happen is a major market crash/correction right when you need to start using the money. This is return sequence risk.

Now that we've reacquainted ourselves with the risks we transfer via SBP, let's run some numbers, shall we? These numbers are for the scenario in which the military member and spouse decide to purchase a $1 million, 20-year term life policy instead of selecting SBP. Any time we attempt to model the future, we have to make assumptions. So, let's get them on the table.

- Military member is male and retires at age 47 with 25 years of service. Spouse is female and is age 45. The numbers don't change that much if the reverse is true.
- Military member's retirement is "High -3," and coincidently enough, the member retires with exactly 25 years of service and 3 years' time-in-grade
- In the case where military retiree lives for 20+ years after retirement, I used 30-year term policy (instead of the 20-year mentioned above). Generally speaking, it is hard to find anything longer than a 30-year term, and after 30 years, your reduction in retirement pay ends (i.e., you don't pay SBP premiums, so if you did maintain insurance after 30 years, the scale will tip towards SBP). If I had used the 30-year policy for the entire run, it would have made SBP look better.
- I used life insurance rates for a retiring military member in good but not "great" health[91].
- Military retiree invests difference between SBP and term-life policy premium, and receives 7.5% each and every year until death (ignores return sequence risk).
- After death, the proceeds from the life insurance policy and accumulated assets are invested at 7.5% in a portfolio with a standard deviation of 11.10% (this will account for return sequence risk during the distribution phase).
- Throughout the scenario, inflation is a constant 2.5%.

Due to the fact we are replacing SBP with life insurance, I made payments from the surviving spouse's investment portfolio (including life insurance proceeds) equal to the SBP payments, to determine the probability that the life insurance decision is equal to or better than SBP for different survival periods for the non-military spouse.

---

91 Thanks to Debbie Kohn of TriBridge Partners LLC for the insurance quotes.

A trial is successful for the insurance/investment mix if there is a least one penny remaining at the end of the trial period. Conversely, a trial is a failure if it is one penny short. I ran numbers for 10-year intervals plus two ages: (1) age 88, the average of life expectancies for a female who is currently older than 45 (life expectancy increases as we age), and (2) age 93, which is the 30th percentile life expectancy for a female. The probability of failure (100 - probability of success) is the risk you transfer to the government. The results are in the table.

Table B-1: Probability that Term Life Insurance Will __Fail__ to Provide for Your Spouse

Spouse Lives to	Military Member Lives to			
	47	57	67	77 (30 years)
55	1%			
65	8%	1%		
75	38%	29%	1%	
85	58%	67%	62%	5%
88	62%	73%	75%	35%
93	67%	80%	86%	82%

NOTE: The shaded boxes indicate that the spouse dies before the military member; consequently, the insurance is used for other purposes.

What do I take from this? Well as long as your spouse is "below average" and is willing to die prior to his or her life expectancy, you can skip SBP and sleep easily. Otherwise, think long and hard before you turn it down...of course there are some exceptions I've spoken about before, and if they apply to your situation, SBP might not be appropriate.

You Shouldn't Love Your Kids Equally

Let me walk that back. Of course you love your kids equally, but that doesn't mean you should show that love by splitting your GI Bill benefits equally between them. That is because of the way the Tax Code treats different sources of college funding.

As you may know, scholarships are tax free to the student. What you may not know is the rest of the story. Scholarships are tax free *if* they are used for qualified tuition and fees. That means that if your child goes to an in-state school on the GI Bill _and_ receives a scholarship, the scholarship will be income to your child. Whether your child actually pays tax on the income will depend on how much other income your child has and how big the scholarship is.

So, if Junior isn't too bright and probably will never receive a scholarship, but his sister is pretty sharp and probably will get some scholarships then you might want to skew the GI Bill towards Junior and use the scholarships combined with your other savings for his sister. The same may hold true if one of your children goes to a private school or goes out of state[92], and both children are likely to receive scholarships. In this case, you would want to skew the GI Bill towards the private school/out of state child.

Another thing to consider is limitations on scholarships. Some scholarships can only be used for tuition. In this case, the GI Bill is "second to pay" and would only pay for the difference between the scholarship and the total tuition and fees. The VA will still count the time in school the same as if they paid the entire tuition bill.

---

92 Under Section 701 of the "Choice Act," your child may qualify for in-state tuition if your child is a covered individual. A child who lives in the state where the institution of higher learning is located (regardless of his/her formal state of residence) and enrolls in the school within 3 years of the transferor's discharge from a period of active duty service of 90 days or more is a covered individual. However, schools are allowed to have additional requirements that must be met in order for a covered individual to be charged the resident rate.

You won't get credit for the scholarships received and you will use up months of benefits and therefore leave money on the table.

One last thing to keep in mind. Only you can change your GI Bill benefits. If you get hit by a bus, no one will be able to change the beneficiary designation after your passing.

Gift Appreciated Assets

Let's say you planned ahead and when Junior was born, you bought 100 shares of IBM stock to pay for college. Well, even though it seems like Junior was born just last week, he is about to head off to school. You could sell the IBM stock and use it to pay for his college. That might be a mistake. When you sell the stock, you'll pay capital gains tax. For most people reading this book, you'll pay 15% on those long-term capital gains. If, on the other hand, you gift[93] the stock to Junior, you might be able to save on some taxes. When Junior sells the stock, he could potentially be in the 10% or 15% marginal tax bracket, and if this is the case, his tax rate on long-term capital gains is 0%.

Now, the IRS is anything but stupid, and there is a limit to this tactic. If a child has more than $2,100[94] in investment income, then the amount over $2,100 is taxed at the parents' tax rate. That doesn't mean you can only gift $2,100, but the capital gains (when combined with any other investment income) shouldn't exceed $2,100 to take full advantage of this technique.

Remember, a gift is a gift is a gift is a gift. Once you gift the stock to Junior, he can decide to use the stock to run off and join the circus. You can't stop him from using the stock to do that, and you can't take the stock back. Of course, you're not required to give Junior a gift next year…

---

93 As of this writing (2017) you can gift up to $14,000 without any gift tax ramifications or a requirement to file a gift-tax return. Remember, the gift must be a gift of a present interest.

94 In 2017.

Hire Junior

If you are self-employed, you might want to consider giving Junior a job. By employing Junior, you transfer income at your assumed higher tax rate to his lower tax rate. Additionally if your business is a sole proprietorship or partnership[95] in which each partner is a parent of the child, and your child is under age 18, you won't have to pay Social Security taxes on your child. Finally, if the child is under age 21, Federal unemployment taxes are waived as well. Your child must be paid a reasonable wage. It can't be too much and it can't be too little.

If Junior is a late bloomer, there might be another option. Employers can set-up Educational Assistance programs and pay up to $5,250[96] for an employee's education. This payment is tax deductible to the employer and is not taxable income to the employee. Unfortunately, dependents are considered a member of the "limitation class," and it is unlikely that you'll be able to take advantage of the benefit if Junior is your dependent. That is why I said it might apply if Junior is a late bloomer. If Junior goes to college or grad school and is no longer a dependent, then you might be able to take advantage of this program. If you have multiple employees, you might have to provide this benefit to all of them, which may make it a little less attractive.

Launder Money

Did I just say that? I don't actually mean launder money, but you may be able to reduce your college expenses by the use of state income tax laws. Thirty-four states and the District of Columbia[97]

---

95 The IRS does not recognize LLCs as an entity. If you form an LLC, you must choose which to be taxed as: a sole proprietorship/partnership or a corporation. This will determine how you will apply this rule.

96 2017.

97 The following states have a state income tax and do _not_ offer a tax deduction or credit: California, Delaware, Hawaii, Kentucky, Massachusetts, Minnesota, New Hampshire, New Jersey, and Tennessee.

offer tax deductions or credits against your state income tax for money contributed to the state-sponsored 529 plan. This means that if you live in Virginia, you must contribute to the VA 529 plan to get the deduction. If you contribute to a 529 plan at USAA or some other broker, you won't get the deduction.

And here is the good part, most of these states don't have a minimum "time-limit" that you must meet to get the deduction. In other words, you could deposit the money today, pay for college tomorrow, and deduct the contribution on this year's tax return. You will need to check your state's rules though, as some states do have a 1-year waiting period on withdrawals.

ACKNOWLEDGEMENTS

Maj Gen Gary Harencak, Sue Thompson and Kymberli Speight who reviewed early editions of this book and provided valuable feedback.

Debbie Kohn who provided life Insurance information to conduct the SBP versus life insurance calculations

Made in the USA
Coppell, TX
25 August 2022